Poems by The Red Neck Poet

Brion L. Morse

POEMS BY THE RED NECK POET

iUniverse books may be ordered through booksellers or by contacting:

iUniverse
1663 Liberty Drive
Bloomington, IN 47403
www.iuniverse.com
1-800-Authors (1-800-288-4677)

ISBN: 978-1-4917-4087-3 (sc)
ISBN: 978-1-4917-4088-0 (e)

Library of Congress Control Number: 2014917491

Print information available on the last page.

iUniverse rev. date: 03/31/2015

Contents

Co-workers Stink

Ever notice your co-workers; the ones that seem to know it all.
The ones who puff themselves up and seem to be at least 10 feet tall;
The ones that know all the answers before you even ask;
The ones that will tell you anything and everything about any given
    task;
The ones that are half your age, but act like they are at least a
    hundred;
To acquire all of that experience and knowledge, it often makes you
    wonder.
The ones that will point a finger or be glad to throw you under
    the bus;
The ones that hate the world and themselves and constantly swear
    and cuss;
The ones that will "ha-ha" you and even seem to sass;
The ones that someday you hope to see fall upon their ass.
The ones that think they are superman and they even think they can
    take a bullet;
But if you listen really hard you can see that they are full of shit.
The ones that say "should of, could of or would of", "Done this or
    that" and thinks he is much smarter;
But when it is all said and done; he could not walk on water.
I am known for speaking my mind or telling you what I think, oh but
    don't get me wrong,
Because I know that my shit does stink.
For me I don't know it all and I never will,
So if you don't have a word of encouragement or a helping hand;
Then keep your damn mouth still.
So when you think you have made your point with your
    comment won;
Try to remember all the wrong you have done and why God gave
    his son.

Goldie the Mom Dog

She was shy and pregnant when she showed up on that summer's
   morn.
Looking for a handout and a place for her pups to be born.
I was not quite ready for anymore mouths to feed;
Two dogs already were quite enough for me.
I made sure she had food and water as I went off to my work;
And when I came back in the evenings, she was waiting at the gate
   with a smiling smirk.
I guess you could say she won my heart, she adopted me;
And bore me six fine pups that summer, in all her glory to be.
She nursed those pups and cared for them; she was a very
   good mom;
But the time eventually comes when they need to find a home of
   their own.
It is not that easy to decide who stays or who must go;
But you make a choice somehow the heart seems to know.
The pups went easily. They were quite cute and furry.
I often wonder did they get good homes or why I even worry.
Now we go for rides in my old pick-up truck.
With the mom dog and two of her boys; hoping to spot a rabbit with
   any luck.
The joy that they give me is way beyond compare.
So when a pregnant stray shows up at your gate; there is no need to
   despair
Open your heart to be adopted if you dare.

How to Get Started Selling Real Estate

I have worked a lifetime or so it would seem;
To pay the bills, be responsible and do what seems to be the right
thing.
My age is catching up to me; I'm no longer the pup I once was.
The aches and pains are more frequent now, but there no need to
make a fuss.
I would like to be retired and throw away the clock;
But our system won't allow that as long as I can walk.
To be approved for disability they say I must quit my job;
Then hope that it gets approved; while I'm forced to steal and rob.
I have worked and saved all my life; to have a place to call a home.
Now with the recent mortgage crisis; the bank wants to foreclose on
my loan.
I have worked hard all my life to see that ends would meet.
Now the ones that would decide my fate want to throw me to the
street.
I guess I'll find a "Maytag" box to call my new home.
Now that I an old and gray; I'll have the time to roam.
I'll have to put up a new mailbox down at the appliance store;
And hope my mail gets delivered to my new "Maytag" box outside
the back door.
Now that my new housing problems are solved; I'll have to figure out
how to eat.
I guess I could dumpster dive at Denny's or pan handle on the street.
I guess I could become a contractor and build cardboard boxes on
the river.
While I wait for my disability to be approved and a donor is found for
a brand new liver.
In the meantime while I wait and ponder the days away in my
cardboard condo;

I wonder how Obama lives his life while he's flying off to
    Mambajambo.
I think it is wrong of me to judge how he should live.
It would be nice though if he could find more to give.
Me...I can't fly anywhere; the money I seem to lack.
While I walk the streets to my cardboard condo, with my fifth of jack.
Oh, it's not that bad though, I have new neighbors buying cardboard
    condos on the river.
At $5.00 a box, I should be able to retire soon or at least buy myself
    a new liver.
Oh wouldn't that be grand to buy a new liver
And live my life in my cardboard box somewhere by the river.

Recession or Depression

"Recession" or "Depression", you call it what you will.
As for me, I see the worried faces, the vacant stores and the
foreclosed houses at the top of the hill.
The politicians we elected; fighting for their jobs;
With new promises of prosperity; while they continue to cheat and rob.
To balance the budgets; the more money that they need.
The salaries they obtain, by our backs, through their lust and their greed.
Oh it would seem quite so joyous the money that they spend;
But when my pockets are empty; there seems none to lend.
We have bailed out the auto companies to have a nice car to drive;
But without a job to drive it to, it's just hard to stay alive.
Our children are our future, on them it would seem sure;
That if we should overcome these problems, it will be for God to find
a cure.
Our economy is collapsing; oh the wars that we wage;
We tend to fight everyone else's battles while history adds a page.
The American dream we once fought for; now seems a thing of the
past.
At least for the working man without a job to grasp.
The rich and the wealthy go on with their money and their greed;
While the poor and the hungry fight always for some need.
America the great was once a good place;
Me being a veteran; I now hang my head with disgrace.
No-one seems to care. It seems "it's all about me".
A nation once as one; I no longer see.
We are selling our freedoms to the ones that will pay;
While the working man works just to survive the basics from day
to day.
God in all your mercy, I know you must have a plan;
I for one don't want to live in this "my own country", when it's run by
China or Iran.

The Mirror

When you look in the mirror
Do you like what you see?
Or do you ask yourself
Who is this person staring back at me?
From freckled face lad to gray haired old man.
The years in between you stared back with a plan.
The wisdom and knowledge that come only through time;
You have always been there with me come reason or rhyme.
Not always knowing of what new adventure would bring,
but always with me come winter to spring.
Like my shadow on a bright sunny day
to make mischief by my side or just lead the way.
You have taught me much through the years of my life.
I have tried to lose you at times due to troubles or strife.
You are a hard one to know even at times hard to see;
that reflection in the mirror staring back at me.
You know all my thoughts the secrets we've shared;
the joy, the pain and at times the only one that cared.
When we shall part our ways and be no more as one.
When my last breath departs me; I shall miss you old friend.
I hope that God shall accept you in his kingdom to be;
as my spirit leaves the body for his glory to see.

Withered Hands

These hands are bent and gnarled from years of work and pain
I remember when a younger man's hands were steady with the reigns
The things that once were easy now take more time and planning to get done.
These old hands have earned the scars and pain for the prizes they have won.
They have carved out sticks of beauty for the kids to walk with on a path.
They have pointed to a new direction or some daunting task.
They have been hard as iron when there was a fight;
Kind and gentle when the time was right.
They have worked hard and served me well throughout all the years.
To spank a butt when needed or wipe a crying tear.
They have showed me comfort too with a caring pet;
With a pat on the head or a hug around a deserving neck.
These hands have made a living and done amazing things.
Now their old and withered with the cold of winter.
I will warm them by the fire and wait for the thaw of spring.
They have cut and chopped my wood to keep these old bones warm.
Now their old and withered they can do no harm.
They hold the pen that I write these words for someone else to see and read.
For a future generation to work with their hands and see the fruits of their deeds.
I would like to leave my kin some legacy for all my aches and pains.
So the years of my life and these withered hands were not at all in vain.

A Better Plan

Plenty to do I just can't get it done.
I'm old and now hurt more; believe me, it isn't fun.
The simple tasks that were once easy are now put to the side.
I hope I can gain the energy to do them, if not, I'll take it in stride.
I'll do what I can; the list keeps getting longer.
I wish there was a miracle pill that I could take to be once again
    stronger.
The strength I once had, now I do lack.
At times I feel and, probably look, like a wet paper sack.
I keep taking the pills that the Doctor says I must take to feel better.
But feel like the paper sack just keeps getting wetter.
I have acquired all of these aches and pains working for
    another man.
If only I was young once again; I would have a better plan.
How that would work, I'm not really sure.
So now I fight my ailments in hopes for a cure.
That would be nice to live my life without pain.
To free my life of my wet paper bag and be able to take a walk out in
    the rain.
To be able to do the things I once done with ease;
To build something with my hands to give to someone to please.
The projects will be put on hold
As I sit here in my rocker and keep getting old.
I'll sit and reflect of when I was a younger man.
Damn it! I wish I would somehow, had a better plan.

Lead Foot Tweeker

I drive a truck from dusk to dawn. It doesn't pay much and I want to
   be back at home.
Nowhere to go to; not many jobs these days.
So round and round I go as I fight the road rage.
Lots of pissed off people trying to get back to their homes. Oh shit!
   There goes another middle finger!!
As I sit in the cab of this truck and smell the last fart linger.
I follow the lead truck on to the paver,
But the only way to catch Dave is if he signed a waiver.
Dave is a special kind of guy or so he seems to think.
Some might even say that his shit doesn't stink.
That doesn't seem to matter at all that much to me.
I just want to stop this truck so I can take a pee.
Round and round we go. Boy I am really getting tired.
I'll have to ask Dave for some of those little white pills, so I also can
   get wired.
Round and Round we go, Isn't this a bitch.
We bust our asses just to pay our bills, while the boss keeps getting
   rich.
Round and round we go, I hang my head in sorrow.
Oh what's that you say, it's Friday and we have to work tomorrow?
Back to the plant we go.
Where trucks are backed up in a row.
Silo #1 they must save for the lead foot tweeker they call Dave.
Oh the chit chat that they say.
The lead foot tweeker is on his way.
Get out of his way here he comes.
The lead foot tweeker is going to show us how it's done.
Driving off into the setting sun;
The lead foot tweeker just showed us why he is number 1.

Lead Foot Tweeker Meets John Part 2

The Lead foot tweeker just snapped an axel. They say that John is on
   the way.
He is the shop mechanic, an angry man throughout the day.
Stay out of his way if at all you have a chance.
But if not, you'd better have a damn good story or go through his
   song and dance.
Boy he is pissed off now. I think he's about to strangle poor Dave's
   neck.
But maybe it's up to Dave to keep his ass in check.
Ol' John works hard to keep the trucks rolling out the door.
He is irritated and pissed off all the time like a festered sore.
I made a mess at the crusher; Bill says I must pin my gate.
No pins to be found in the truck; so now I must face Johns hate.
I think ol' John won't be living long with all that anger and hate.
I just hope he doesn't die while looking for pins for my gate.
I do not want to be responsible for that ol' man's death.
If anything, I should hope that the boss would smell the whisky on
   his breath.

Molded

There is only one you, like it or not, you are unique.
Like a snowflake, no two are the same.
Like a finger print, there should be no shame.
You are what you are, there's no need to find fault.
A diamond that sparkles as the sun hits its facets, you too have many
assets.
Don't regard yourself useless or without any worth.
God gave you your image, it started at birth.
Love who you are; be an example to all.
There is no need that you should feel small.
Walk through this life with your head held to the sky.
God is watching you from somewhere on high.
Do your best in this life, there is a price on your head.
God will pay the bill when you become dead.
You are a shell formed from a mold; not to be bought or to be sold.
A unique specimen from the day you were born to the day you
grow old.
So live your life well; do the best that you can.
God broke that mold when you were born, he has a plan.
It's not just about this life, but do good while you're here.
So you can live a better life in his kingdom when there will be no
more tears.

The Mask

Life is a stage we are all actors as we struggle through life.
You can be whoever you want to be, Shakespeare with a play or
    Brutis with a knife.
How well can you act, do you really want the part?
Can you lie well enough to make a new start?
It should be quite easy for the ones who can lie the best.
Who will put on the mask and give it a test?
As the curtain goes up and the drama unfolds;
How will you perform for the message to be told?
We all like to be entertained; everyone loves a story.
Can you act well enough to make it sound gory?
Didn't you once cry wolf? Was it really there?
Or was it a lie intended to scare.
You wear the mask well. It shows what you're really worth.
But for me I'd rather see the play with the mask that was given to you
    at your birth.
You wear the mask well; you have made fools of many.
The stage has paid well for your acting with a great many pennies.
You act quite well with quite a story to tell.
Is it the truth or another scene from the stage; are we all doomed to
    hell?

Wake Up Call

There once was a time in America when goods were made by an
American.
And the products that they made were marked "Made in the USA";
not stamped "Made in Japan".
The pride in America is gone now; at least it would seem to be.
The products that once were made here in the USA are now shipped
to us by the way of the sea.
Our economy and way of life is collapsing it's not hard to see why.
We outsource our livelihoods to have their crap to buy.
It would seem that we can't make it ourselves the prices they are too
high.
So we'll have to keep having it built in China so we can have their
crap to buy.
I was born an American; that doesn't mean much anymore.
The things that once were made here are being shipped right back
to us;
As the ships wait to be unloaded at the docks down by the shore.
The jobs are all gone. The factories are all shut down.
The streets are empty; there's nothing left of this town.
The prosperity we once knew; it is now shipped to some other soil.
It was once in our land where great things were done here as we
labored and we toiled.
We are a nation of people who always want more.
The people that have and the people who have nothing and are
always poor.
Towns grew and they prospered when the work was there.
Now that the gold is all gone; the cupboards are bare.
Our economy is run by our resources; its supply and demand.
Built by the working man with his mighty hands.
The rich and the greedy will use what they must
To acquire more wealth through their power and their lust.

Wake up America before it's too late
Our country is decaying at an alarming rate.
We must bring our jobs back to American soil;
So we can once more be a proud country and not continue to watch
    our country spoil.
How can we do this? We must have a plan.
We cannot continue to put our trust into one man.
God save our country; our trust is in your hands.
Make us free and prosperous once again; as we put on the armor of
    your word; as we take a stand
To fight for our rights and freedom in this great land.

Brat or Bastard

Ever noticed the kids these days; the crap they wear? The jewelry, the
    piercings; it really is a shame.

Oh to hear the parents say let them show their identity; when it is
    really all their blame.

There is no respect anymore. It is society of entitlement for the little
    bastards.

They throw a fit to have it now and call you everything under the sun
    if they aren't accommodated by their last words.

And the language that they speak it's enough to make a saint out of
    a sailor.

Oh, and the clothes they wear it makes me want to become a tailor.

I would sew a pair of britches that fit above the waist.

So the little bastards wouldn't trip or fall while he's trying to hold his
    pants up as he runs from a policeman in a chase.

Oh that bling and glitter hanging from his face.

It makes me want to grab a handful in a fight.

As I do some corrective rearranging to make his face look right.

And the music they listen to, they call it rap.

The language that they call singing, I say it's nothing but crap.

It's all about kill this or kill that; your sister being a hoe.

So much hate and guile that I just don't know.

And you would think that they are deaf,

As you hear their damn car stereo a block away, as you try to catch
    your breath.

The innocence of childhood has all been taken away by computers
    and cell phones.

But who am I to say. As they fill their minds with images and songs.

I have to wonder about those parents who think their child could do
    no wrong.

Our jails and our prisons are full of this kind of thinking;

Of the children of parents that were given no guidance or discipline
to the little bastards when a hand should have been risen.

How do you correct a society running out of control?

Just sit back and watch it or try to correct a dysfunctional child as he
takes his stroll off to the prison gates.

He will try the system out as the dysfunctional child is lead to his
prison cell with an all mighty shout.

Now the parents sit and wonder who is to blame as the dysfunctional
child awaits the gallows; now isn't that a shame.

Buying a Used Car

Relationships are like buying a car.

Take the test drive first; before the sticker shock or the emotional scar.

You had better like the make and model; before you park it in the yard.

Because if you don't and want to return it; you will find it very hard.

So take the test drive first, drive it around the block for a while.

If you don't; there won't be any returning it for a better model.

You will soon be stuck with a great big ol' pile.

If you like the make and model and want to make the payment;

Remember this one may or may not last a lifetime.

Is it worth the money spent?

For me, I'll keep taking the test drive in hope I find the model I like.

Before I park it in the garage and make a payment and know that it's right.

This make and model is old with many miles and looks like a piece a crap.

Not many want a classic that's good for one more lap.

So make sure you like the make and model and the condition it is in.

Before you park it in your bed to take it for a spin.

Horn Dog Don't Learn

You look like my Ex; do you want to play house for a while?
Then when the fun is all over we can call it quit.
Then we can call the lawyers in to see what each other will get.
Will you suck the life blood from me so I won't be able to pay my
    rent?
Or will it be the best ride I ever had for the money spent?
Do you want to play house, you look like you would be fun.
Do you want to be my next Ex or take off on the run?
Do you want to play house without all the drama?
Or will you be my next ex and run home to your mama.
Let's go for a ride; are you ready for the test?
Are you qualified for the job to be my next ex?
I'll pay all your bills; there will be nothing left for me.
Do you want to be my next Ex; let's try it and see.
You will be living the good life with money to spare.
Do you want to be my next Ex; let's try it if you dare?
Do you want to be my next ex; you will have money to burn.
As you send me to the poor house for a lesson I must learn.
Living alone seems the best life for me.
There will be no more next ex; you just wait and see.
Oh wait! Who's that walking into the store?
Looks like my next Ex; maybe I'll score.
Hey there; you look mighty fine.
Would you like to go out somewhere to dine?
I'll plot my next beauty to be.
Damn, why these women won't let me be free.

Message from Home

I write the letters and poems to my daughter in prison, she looks
    forward to them, often with a smile and maybe a tear.
For a short time at least I hope they will inspire and wipe away the
    bad memories of her life she has endured throughout the years.
It gripes me plenty to know they a censored and read by a few.
They were intended for one, not for the whole damn crew.
I know they are doing their job, so don't abuse that power and title
    that you've been given.
Remember it's a job and how you make a living.
Remember too we all make a mistake here and there along the way.
So have a heart also, don't be so harsh to judge. Who are you to say?
There will be a time of judgment we will all have to answer to
    someday.
When the book of life is opened to your name; what then will
    you say?
It seems I have gained some celebrity with the inmates and the crew.
So I'll keep on writing; who the hell would have knew.
A celebrity, not really, I am just a man;
Who tries to leave a message with my poems for those that read to
    understand?
Words that are written seem to have more power than those that are
    spoken;
So read and enjoy the messages, so you too can be awoken.

Vacation With a View or Just Screwed

Welcome back from your vacation. Did your hosts accommodate you
  well?
Did you like your visit at the grey bar hotel?
Did you have a beach front property of a sliver for a view?
Did you enjoy the friend you meet or did they leave a bad taste in
  your craw for upon it you must chew?
You left in such a hurry, you didn't even say goodbye.
I was left here at home just wondering why.
You left your sunglasses and your sunscreen; you were gone long
  enough to get a tan.
Did your hosts accommodate you well or did you wish you were in
  Iran?
Did you make any new friends that might be worth talking about?
Or did they leave in a hurry also and not give their loved ones so
  much as a shout.
Did you get to do and see all the things that the tour guide foretold?
You were gone long enough now that I am getting old.
Did you do all the tourist things? Did you get to see all the sights?
Or did your tour guides and the brochure about your vacation
  destination leave you with little or no rights.
Did you learn any new languages while in this foreign land?
Did you get to go swimming and get to dip your toes into the sand?
Was this the vacation you really planned and saved for "The vacation
  of your dreams"?
Or a childhood nightmare that awakened you with a mighty scream.
The next time you decide to take a vacation I hope that you will
  choose your destination a little better
And choose a place with a better view and the beaches are a little
  wetter.

Rich Man – Poor Man

Do you feel like an asset or just an ass?
To be used for someone else's benefit and taken for a ride;
Pushed into a corner or shoved to the side.
The hired hand does his job and takes all the flack;
While the silver spoon takes all the credit and then turns his back.
The hired hand wishes he could afford what money could bring.
He pays his bills with nothing left in the pot from winter to spring.
The silver spoon has plenty, but there's nothing to give.
While he lives in his mansion; he should come and see how I live.
I love my little home that I struggle to keep.
Yes, at times I do hang my head and weep.
I think of the riches that the silver spoon seems to have.
This time I'll hang my head and laugh.
He will never know the riches I know and fill every day.
The love of my God as he shows me a better way.
So the hired hand will be thankful for the riches he has.
The ones the silver spoon will never be able to purchase with all his
    money.
The ones I'll see with my god someday in the land of milk and honey.

Life's Journey

Why does it take a lifetime to see and write the wrongs that we have done?
I cannot say for sure the lessons we have won.
The wisdom and knowledge we must learn and acquire.
To pass down to our loved ones to prevent them from becoming a
    thief or a liar.
I have traveled the road of life with all the hills and valleys in between.
Oh the things I have learned and the things I have seen.
God shows me things he has freely given.
The real things that matter most and why his son was risen.
The beauty of life and the simple joys that surround.
The stillness of a clear mountain lake at sunrise without a sound.
The beauty of a mountain meadow that blooms flowers in the spring;
To the beauty of snow that winter will bring.
The laughter of child as they run off to play.
Take a look at these joys there here to see every day.
The turmoil and sadness are here also; we must live it to our best;
As we learn and acquire the wisdom and knowledge of life's mighty quest.
We all have our own journey with no real map to follow.
We might take the wrong road a few times with the pill hard to swallow.
These are the lessons we must learn as we travel.
The road may be paved, but most of it will be gravel.
Take a break a few times to see where you have been.
There is more to life, just touch his hem.
Be grateful for what you have, the journey may be long and hard.
Learn from your past as you struggle for another yard.
You will grow old and gray with stories of your journey through your life.
Pass on the knowledge and wisdom to your children so they have
    less struggle and strife.
Teach of the beauty of God's goodness and his spirit that surrounds
    us each day.
The lessons of life and how to pray.

Thieves at the Pump

I go to the pump to fill up my car. I get less and less for my money. I
   can't go very far these days.
I have to get to work so I can buy less with my money. The boss says
   he won't give me a raise.
We are all slaves to the pump. The oil companies have you by the
   cajones.
While the CEO's make their six figure incomes, dress in their fine
   Italian suites, drive their nice cars.
Oh what a bunch of phonies.
Let's see what I can sacrifice this month so I can make the ol'
   paycheck stretch a little farther.
I need meds, the dogs need to eat, and I need electricity and water.
Let's see how I can make a few extra bucks.
I could go up on the corner at Wal-Mart or Pilot and panhandle with
   any luck.
I'll make me a sign it will say Homeless down on my luck.
And as you drive by, you can throw me a buck.
I'll wear my crappiest clothes and not shave for a while. Ill grow my
   hair out a little longer.
I'll look and act the part, I'll look very shitty.
Oh I'll play the part so you will show pity.
Homeless, stranded, need gas for my car. Whatever sign that might
   work.
So I can play on your pity, so you won't feel like a jerk.
I'll give the money right back to the clerk at the pump;
So I have gas another week and hear the boss say jump.
I'll say Yes- um boss, how high would you like? As high as the sky or
   the prices at the pump?
You will feel warm and fuzzy as you throw me a buck or two.
You will thank your lucky charms that this is not you.
Be grateful, my friend, as you drive into the pumps.

If you can afford to suck down a few more gallons to get by.
I'll salute the oil companies with one finger and shake my head why.
It's all about greed and political power.
I hope they won't shut my water off;
I didn't pay the bill and I'm getting kind of stinky and could really use
a shower.
The boss keeps asking me why I smell and look like shit.
I just laugh and grin and say; you won't give me a raise,
So I have to stretch my paycheck to somehow make it fit.

Blood is Red. Skin Isn't

Are you regarded by your employer and co-workers as someone with
little worth?

Are you treated like a piece of crap because of the color of your
birth?

Are you talked down to as if you had no brain at all?

Can you perform the tasks asked of you without being made to feel
small?

By the ones who judge you for whatever indifference

You may have or maybe you're too skinny, too fat or too tall?

If you care to judge someone, then judge their deeds and substance
of their worth.

Not the color of their skin they were given at their birth.

None of us choose our parents or had a say so in our birth.

The attitudes were developed on down the road, as well as the fat
around our girth.

Me, I was born a poor white child.

Where I was raised and my attitude of life put the red about my neck.

The things we learn, the things we do seem to mold us into who we
are, by heck.

As you travel through your life, try to see who and what you are.

Will you point your finger? Will that take you far?

We are a world of many colors; a world of many creeds.

Wouldn't it be great if we could be a world without lust or greed?

Brain Fart

I can't think of much to write about my thoughts seem to have
    run dry.
Like a drought stricken stream bed with no water from the sky.
The thoughts are not flowing the well seems to be dry.
I can't come up with a subject; no matter how hard I try.
My fan club will be disappointed if I can't get on the ball.
The thoughts are all empty; there is nothing at all.
The Rolodex between my ears; for some reason it seems it has shut
    down.
I don't want the fan club to be empty and have to leave with a frown.
I've been getting sicker; maybe I'll use that for an excuse not to write.
Or I can't refill the ink on the printer, because money is too tight.
No, the fan club deserves better than that.
But for now the car is empty and running on a flat.
The poems go to my kids and the poorest fan club on earth.
I don't get a dime from them; I can't seem to fatten any of my girth.
I keep asking for money as I send off a letter,
But like the drought stricken stream bed, nothing seems to be
    getting any wetter.
What is the fan club going to do when my child comes home?
How will they take it then when there won't be another poem?
They will adjust to the issues as life to must move on.
They too will someday leave for home.
But I hope they will remember mail call. Moriah's dad and a hand
    written poem.
P.S. Send Money

Clown Around Now or Clown Around Later

The elections are over, what do you think?
Did your party win; is the ship about to sink?
The political ads; boy am I glad they are over at last!
Well, it is four more years of nothing and empty promises of an
    election once past.
I didn't vote this year. I didn't see the need.
I'm pissed off enough of the lies and the greed.
It's not about our country that should be clear to see.
It's all about special interests; how they will profit; not you and me.
These past few years I have steadily watched our country go to shit.
It seems to be the new normal of an eloquently speaking though a
    dim whit.
I recently went to get some old barn wood of a diary of the past.
I found two old railroad ties that were spiked with spikes
With dates from the great depression dated 1929 & 1930.
It made me wonder how much longer will this current one last.
Our current leader had better stop talking out of his ass;
Because from where I sit his mouth is just passing gas.
Now don't get me wrong, I don't want to proclaim doom and gloom,
But my view point, there isn't any more room for the bullshit and
    empty promises with no real relief in sight.
I just hope that when China, North Korea or Iran are knocking at our
    doors with missiles,
We won't have to leave our homes in a plight.
You made your decision when you went to the polls.
You made your choice according to each of their rolls.
Did you vote for the clown present or the clown that would be?
Either way, I think we are doomed. I hope I won't have to see.
Four more years will tell of a story of this once great land.
I hope we won't have to take up arms against our leaders as we take
    a stand.
These political views are solely that of the Red Neck Poet. You figure
    it out.

Fan Club Thank You

As I sit here and read the thank you card that my Fan Club sent;
My heart is melted, it meant so much to me, I often wonder was it
    time well spent.
To see the names and comments though my fan club may be small;
It meant everything to me; I love you each and all.
I don't always get emotional or moved to a tear.
Your card did just that; I'll cherish it through the years.
As the days and years go by I'll think of how my daughter shared
    those poems to my fans.
I hope they moved you also, for your life's to make better plans.
I'll try to keep on writing; though at times it seems hard.
But this time was easy for me and a very special thank you card.
Thank you Fans I'm glad you enjoy a letter with a poem.
Remember the messages between the lines, when you too shall go
    home.
Thanks again

Friend or Foe

You are quite alone in this world from the time of your birth.
The acquaintances, lovers, associates and friends are all of your
    choice
You have to decide what at all they are worth.
The friends you choose and how you live often determine who
    you are.
So choose your friends wisely and hope they take you far.
Choose the losers in your life they will take you far also.
To a deep dark lonely place that many will not want to follow.
There are two types of people; the ones that can help you and the
    ones that will take you down.
The givers and takers that will rob you blind, with the U-Haul loaded
With all of your possessions as its heading out of town.
Give tell it hurts, but never be unguarded.
Let your guard down once, then you will feel unrewarded,
True Friends will love you for what you are and share their lives
    with you.
Like a favorite pair of jeans or a tailored shoe.
Be cautious in life; learn who you can trust.
Pay heed to these words; it could be life or bust.
The devil is deceiving; he can show you all the riches you may desire.
Just make sure of whom you're trusting in before you cash in to
    retire.
He will show you all the kingdoms of this world and tell you they
    could be yours if you but worship him.
My advice for you is choose your friends wisely and tell this one to
    take an everlasting swim.
Into the lake of fire where he shall be no more.
Then we can live our lives eternal with one another; be it rich or poor.

I'm dying for a PB&J

What would you miss most if you lost it all right now?
If you lost your identity and was given a number to be called by.
With no freedom to do the small things you used to love.
Like a PB&J sandwich at midnight with a glass of milk from a cow.
The things you once enjoyed freely are now a thing of the past.
Will you stop and think of where you were and how long will now
    last?
Wouldn't you like to order a cheeseburger and fries with a large
    chocolate shake?
Have you learned yet and paid the price for all of your mistakes?
Are you enjoying your freedom now? Do you miss the things you
    once enjoyed?
A walk along a path with a friend or maybe even an old boss you
    once had
When you were once employed?
The laughter of a child's voice running for a hug
Or the excitement of a new discovery of some sort of bug.
I try to think of the things that I would surely miss; if by magic they
    were to disappear.
Right now they seem mighty to me, but small when Christ shall
    reappear.
The time you spent for a crime committed may be long or may be
    small.
Try to remember what Christ went through and why he died for all.
So as you're craving the things you miss and desire most from your
    prison cell;
Remember why Christ died for you and be grateful you won't burn in
    hell.

Learning to Fly

As I address the envelope to my loved one with a letter and a poem.
I think of the ones that will be touched the most
By what the words say so far away from home.
Does what I say and write have a message to be told?
Or are they of some foolish rambling, man that is just getting old.
Do they really touch a heart?
Do they inspire someone to make a new start?
There is usually a message written between the lines. Listen, see and
    hear.
Ponder these words with an aching heart or maybe a tear.
Words have the power they can hurt or they can heal.
I hope I have done some small part to teach someone not to steal.
Life is too tough already to reap the punishment of a crime.
Like the saying goes, don't do it if you can't do the time.
There is so much to lose in life to have to start from scratch.
Like a fledgling new born eagle awaking from its mother's incubated
    hatch.
You must learn to fly once again and learn to live clean and sober.
And fight the fight of life if you choose to grow any older.
Take the small steps in your life; like a child learning to walk all over.
Like a walk along a stream or maybe finding a four leaf clover.
Enjoy the simple things; forget the past; it won't matter. It will be a
    memory of things gone by.
You keep an eye held to the sky.
Watch for that soaring eagle; it will be a message from above.
Of how you must learn how to fly all over and of God's great love.

Mirror Mirror

Mirror mirror what's that you say?
My daughter is calling; she needs a favor for the day.
Could you watch the kids for a while? Oh no, you will have to find
    another.
After all I'm too important and vain to play grandmother.
Not now, not ever, not even for a while.
Please, I'm too vain, that's just not my style.
You see it's all about me; I'm the vainest one of them all.
Just ask the mirror that hangs up on my wall.
Mirror mirror you say there is another party this weekend. You can
    count me in; I'll do it up right.
I'll be the vain one high as a kite.
Mirror mirror oh the party was fun.
No time for the kids though, as I push them away and how I can shun.
Mirror mirror it's all about me.
What is your problem? Why can't you see?
Mirror mirror don't you judge me; I have no need for that.
I'll lie in my bed eating bon bons, smoke my weed and keep getting fat.
Mirror mirror I have no time for others. I will certainly not find time
    for you.
I'll discard you like my daughter and grandchildren; like a pair of old
    worn out shoes.
Mirror mirror when my children were young they learned of life upon
    their own.
With no help from me, with any instruction ever shown.
I have taught them nothing of how to live their life;
Of how to raise their children or even be a wife.
Mirror mirror what is that finger that you are waiving back and forth?
No, I have no shame within me, you will never make me feel guilty or
    make me feel small.
I'm too great for that; I'm the vainest one of all.

My House

My house is small; it's where I live my life.
I share it with my dogs for I am single, and there is no wife.
I like it this way. I don't often have an argument with my dogs.
They know my moods when I am angry, happy or sad.
I come home they are waiting, with their stubs for tails wagging
    happy to see me; they are mighty glad.
I fix the things in my small house as I can afford to get them done.
I chip away with the list at ten and hope soon to see it down to one.
With each project finished I feel a sense of accomplishment and
    pride.
I put the list down for the time being and set the tools aside.
My small house is not a mansion but it is my castle, my refuge, and
    my home.
I know when I pull through my gate that I am not alone.
Regardless what a day I've had the kids come a running; their happy
    I am home.
I too am glad to see them. We are a family once again and were not
    alone.
My little house gives me shelter, a fire keeps me warm.
The dogs warn me of intruders and protect me from any harm.
I love my little house that I have fought so hard to keep.
I see other little houses with foreclosed signs in their yards; it makes
    me want to weep.
My little house isn't worth what I'm paying for it now. You see, I'm
    under water with the loan,
Because Freddy Mae and Barney Mac had to steal investors' money
To pay for their penthouse suites on Wall Street and a mansion or
    two of their own.

No Brainer

I'm not a smart man, but God gives us each talents of how he
    sees fit.
I have seen and worked for smarter people that were nothing but
    dimwits.
I believe you really don't have to be a super brain to function well or
    run a job or catch a train.
God gave me enough sense with what I have not to stand out in the
    rain.
The older I get my brain seems to forget more; I can't do the tasks as
    I once did.
Now my brain has senior moments. I don't think or remember well as
    I did when I was a kid.
My mind and body are slowing down. Believe me, I feel it every day.
I recall a distant time in my life of a younger man working on a ranch
    and bailing hay.
Age has a way of showing us the things we learn in life.
But for me I have not the brains or the intellect to be able to make a
    living without the hard labor or the strife.
I leave these words of age and wisdom for a younger generation
    to see.
Get an education, learn a skill; make money while you're young and
    able;
not when you're old and broken down like me.

No More Aces

I do not know the impact of the hearts and emotions I have touched
  with the words I have written;
Of how someone so far away could possibly be comforted by my
  words
And think of a better time in their life with the love of a pet such as a
  puppy or a kitten.
Life is always a challenge. There is always a price to pay.
The fan club members will go home also to find a better day.
When you have done your time and it is time to leave.
Think back and remember why and how you got where you are then
  think do I have another ace hid up my sleeve.
No I think not. This time it will be up to you to do the things you
  must
To return to your loved ones and once again win their trust.
We all have our days of sadness, being depressed or just feeling blue.
Hold your head up anyway there is only one you.
Heartache will pass and scars will heal in time.
You will have the freedom you once had before you done the crime.
Few people think of consequences of their actions while they do a
  crime.
It's when they get caught and have to suffer the penalty behind the
  bars as their doing time.
So when you are free and have those days that will bring you to that
  deep dark place;
Think back in your life and stop before you pull that ace.
The deck might not be stacked in your favor, it very seldom is.
Stop and think it through and then think it through again;
Is the cost of the crime worth all the pain?
Everything comes with a price tag. Everyone has their hand held out.
Your freedom is no different to you there now should be no doubt.
What was the price you paid?

Was it worth everything you lost or whatever you have saved?

These questions should be easy to answer they are just yes or no.

Do you have what you once had? Do you have anything at all to
    show?

Don't hang your head in sorrow;

There will once again be a tomorrow.

Realize the things gone by, you can build again.

With what you have put behind you, like the devil.

Now the answer to your life should be win.

The Red Neck Poet, Mechanic, Artist, Grumpy dog man, Mountain
    Man and dad

Old Hat

I just stitched my old straw hat for the next summer's season.
I can't tell you why or give you any sound reason.
I just like my summer hat, like me, it has a certain flare.
Oh new would be nice, but like me, this one shows wear.
Maybe that's why I like it; wear seems to give it character and charm.
Like the cracks in this hat and my face, they can do you no harm.
My old hat can be stitched though, to repair its bad shape.
But the cracks in my face, I think there is no escape.
I'll live with those cracks, they would be too expensive to fix.
I don't think there would be enough plastic anyway to do the trick.
My old hat has done me well, but like me it can't retire.
Come next fall, I probably have to stitch it again, but next time I'll
    have to use bailing wire.
I'll keep on stitching as long as I can stitch this old hat together.
So we can fight off the sun and maybe some bad weather.
This old hat has grown like an appendage; it's kind of nice to have
    around.
And like an appendage I don't think there would be another like it to
    be found.
So I'll keep on stitching this old hat as long as the straw will hold its
    place.
For one more season of work to keep the sun off my face.

Red Neck vs. White Trash

Me, I'm a redneck, as tough it would be.
No need for a discussion this poem is not about me.
Although I could at times look the part.
I'm going to tell you a story about white trash,
So hold on now, here we go, I'm about to start.
It's not hard to spot them; they seem to be everywhere these days.
You can see them at the mini mart buying their beer in a half
    drunken daze.
There's a big difference between white trash and red neck.
White trash cares about nothing in life other than when he gets his
    next welfare check.
The red neck, he does care and will try his best to hold down a job.
White trash won't work unless he has to; this gives him the freedom
    to steal and rob.
White trash will scrap out what he can salvage off someone else's
    property
And thief it right from under your feet. I call it a new way to steal
    and rob.
Then he will take it to his house to strip the good and discard the
    trash in his front yard.
As your property values decline, because of this uncaring piece of lard.
I think we all can easily say we know some white trash we can talk
    about.
You will see them lying on the couch drinking beer and complaining
    that Medicaid didn't cover gout.
A red neck will throw his beer cans into the back of his ol' pick-up
    truck.
White trash will throw them out the front door of the house
And try to hit the overflowing trash can with any kind of luck.
If the red neck is short on money he will try to sell you something of
    value at the local bar.

38

While the white trash will go to the Dollar Loan Center to get his beer
money with the title to his car.

White trash will go to storage auctions to bid on what might become
his next yard sell find.

While his snot nosed kids run around the continual yard sale with a
load in their behind.

But the oinker white trash wife, she doesn't seem to mind.

White trash doesn't seem to have many morals on how they run their
life.

Seems all they want in life is a case of beer and a porky for a wife.

For me I hope to see whitey loading up the U-Haul and moving out.

So I can see my property increase in its value and I can again sing
and shout.

Short Cut – What Short Cut?

I have such a long way to go in hope that I can get it all done.
With little hope of a future of tales to be spun.
I can't find the short cut to the easy road of life no matter how hard
that I try.
Now I am old with little need to wonder why.
This road is rutted and harder to travel;
With many rocks and a whole lot less gravel.
There is much to do before the road comes to an end.
Bills to be paid and no money to spend.
I still need to learn of life's direction of travel.
The easy road that is paved or the hard one that is gravel.
Either way I go there is a lesson to learn.
The good path or the bad path; how must I discern.
Sometimes I think the answers are right before our eyes;
The cloudy dark way or the bright blue skis.
The rocks in the stream might slow the waters travel;
Like the two roads of life; the paved or the gravel.
Eventually the water will reach the river and the river will reach the
ocean.
Your life will have turbulence on its journey with upsets unpredicted
and unseen.
You will carve your nitch out of the sand.
You will make your own mark on the land.
Keep on going with your thoughts never knowing of what might
appear around the next bend.
It could be the rich fertile valley that will produce the crops to sustain
a better life.
If not, maybe the next bend or the next bend.
You won't know until you travel that river to the ocean with struggle
and strife.
Look for the bright star to shine a light for your travel.

Remember there has to be some stones in the stream and rocks to
    make gravel.
Nothing comes easy and sometimes it takes time to carve a canyon
Like the river that runs through it. It started as a stream on its travels.
The pyramids and great wonders were not built overnight.
Keep flowing to the ocean and fight the good fight.

Spud Hates Tweakers

My dog loves to sing as I try to play a tune on my harmonica.
Like me, he can't carry a note, but he tries like he wanna.
He makes me laugh we both share a smile.
Life is all good, at lease for a while.
Spud is his name; he is named after a potato.
He doesn't like my daughter. He wants to chew on her leg; don't you
 know.
He's not really a bad dog, just a little skitso.
He loves and guards me with his life; it makes my daughter jealous
 oh so.
He sleeps with me on my bed and will jump at the ready.
To chew on a leg; you better walk very easy and walk very steady.
My daughter doesn't like him I really don't understand.
She tries to pet him while he chews on her hand.
Stubbie is his brother; they will fight each other to the death.
As I try to break them apart; I can barely catch my breath.
They both get a little shock therapy at this time with the cattle prod;
To gain each respect and save me a vet bill from Dr. ROB.
He is a one person dog; my protector and security alarm.
He is not really vicious; he really means no harm.
He's just doing his job;
Don't steal from me and don't try to rob.
He has the right to take a piece out of your ass;
Just stay out of my yard you white tweaker trash.
If Spud takes you down in my yard, you better make it over the fence
 on the run.
If you don't, Ill zap you with the cattle prod just to see you light up
 for fun.
Stay out of my yard! Don't ever try to steal from me.
Next time you will have a shot gun up your ass; try it again and
 you'll see.

The Future Depends on You

I lay here on my bed; it's where I try to find the words of inspiration to
   write about.

As I put my thoughts to paper I wonder as to the ones that will read
   these words,

I'm just venting my emotions, is it therapy without a shout?

Do these words really matter or do they make any sense at all?

I believe words do have an impact, you see it every day;

News in print, books, magazines, and messages upon a wall.

It is the written form of communication put down for someone to
   read and see.

Maybe written instructions; to a bathroom of where to take a pee.

All forms of communication written for future generations to be
   taught.

A lesson, a song or a poem. An easy message with a rhyme that will
   take a little time

to decipher with or without any given thought.

I hope for that future generation that these words were not given in
   vain.

That I gave some form of message for someone to have some gain.

I see upon a book or a magazine a price tag that you must pay to
   read.

I guess it is the way of life to fill somebody's needs.

I too would like to acquire some green to fill my bank account.

It doesn't matter the denomination; it could be any amount.

I don't know, are my writings really worth the ink and paper it takes
   to write the words?

Will the future readers be grateful or just a few degenerate turds?

I don't know I really don't want to offend.

I don't write these words to acquire any wealth at all or to be able to
   afford a box of Depends.

Yes, I am old and at times afraid to fart.

For the fear that I will fill my drawers, then I won't feel very smart.
And yes it has happened, the world won't end.
Please send money!!!! I need another box of Depends.
Oh my, I see a future for me now with my fan club
And endorsement checks that will never end.
As I put on another diaper and open a new box of Depends.

This Child

There was once a child that grew up on her own.

The things that she needed most in life were for varied reasons were never shown.

The things that matter most like love, understanding, guidance and wrong from right.

No child should have to learn of these things; while their mother is off getting high as a kite.

A child shouldn't have to learn what seems normal from watching a program on T.V.

They should be taught by a loving parent that says come on, let's go and see.

A child shouldn't have to learn of life watching their mother stumble from a bar

With her drunken lover, as they make it to their car.

A child shouldn't have to enjoy life rambling through the desert to find a playmate to make a friend.

Like a horned toad lizard or a tortoise. Because they had no mother on that they could depend.

No child should be locked up in their room while their mother and lover are getting high.

And when they open the door they are beaten if they inquire why.

No child should have to fend on their own with no food to be found;

While their mother spends her days at the local bar; as the losers buy another round.

If a child should have to learn the lessons of life from what they see or hear;

It shouldn't have to be of their mother saying to her lover; "Let's have another beer".

As this child grows; what lessons has she learned?

Of how a dysfunctional life with another dysfunctional lover and how to live life burned.

This child grew and became a mother of her own.
But this child learned a lesson from all the hurt, because the love
was never shown.
This child grew to teach her kids the things she never had;
And of a happier better way to raise her children and why they all
should be glad.
It takes a lifetime to see and learn of the damage done.
This child has learned the hard way; as she watches her children play
and run.
A poem for this child of mine
I couldn't be prouder.
Love dad.

Two Tone Paint Job

I don't know what is around the corner or what path will take me to
another place.

I worry about the bills being paid the responsibilities of life that put
more white upon my head and face.

The passage of time has done its job and done it well.

I'll have to buy a box of just for Men and get the hot babe in the
commercial so she won't know or be able to tell.

Yes, with time come the rewards of white upon my head and face.

They tell me of things I have worried about as I have served my time
in life in the human race.

Wouldn't it be nice if you had a crystal ball that you could gaze in and
it would tell you all?

So you wouldn't have to worry so much about tomorrow as you're
caught up in the pace

As you look in the mirror and see more white upon your head and
face.

I don't know what tomorrow brings; I'll keep buying the bottle in
the box,

So I can be young once more and play with Goldie lox.

Oh crap, it's not working anymore.

I have a two tone paint job upon my head and face.

The hot babe has caught on to my age, now I score no more.

Waiting to Be Called

I sit here in the lobby of the Veterans hospital waiting for my appointment.
I look around me and see the faces of other veterans and I think of
why this country is free.
I wonder these were the lucky ones the ones that made it home,
Like me the faces tell a story of lives battles and the scars they
acquired on their own,
I look upon these people and I see much more than a face.
I see the men and women who gave their all in another place.
I give thanks to God now that I am free and know my name was not
engraved in a slab of granite that they call the wall.
As I sit here waiting for my name to be called.
I talk to a Veteran he tells me they replaced a valve in his heart.
He was a little tender from the procedure, but was looking forward to
a new start.
He told me how he lay there in his hospital bed in a coma with life
support.
With his family gathered round on his birthday with a cake.
Of how he seen and spoke to his deceased father and was told this
was not yet his wake.
At that time my name was called. I wanted to speak with this person more
Of what he seen while in his coma of life on a distant shore.
This man was gone when I left the room.
I stopped to collect my thoughts and I wondered would this man see
his father soon?
Perhaps not on native soil, but of an entirely other place.
It made me stop and ponder and remember also of my own father
and how I miss his face.
Then I stopped and realized it is because of like me these men and
women fought and gave for all of us on that there is no doubt.
I hope that when I am finally called to that other place.
I hope I can perhaps once again gaze upon my father's face.

What is Normal

I'm a back hills hillbilly, red neck son of a bitch;
Trying to pay my bills; with no easy fix.
The new normal isn't working. Food stamps don't go that far.
No money for gas to put in the car.
The kids are all growing with need for new clothes.
There old stuff is worn and patched from many holes.
Our jobs have been outsourced to China and Japan.
Maybe I can find a new job in the missile industry and work for Iran.
No jobs here. The food lines keep getting longer.
I think the new normal is making families stronger.
But I'm a back hill hillbilly, red neck son of a bitch.
I'll do what it takes to keep a roof over my head, keep the family fed
    and have lights on with a flip of a switch.
The new norm is not working from what I see;
Unless struggling from day to day, taking handouts or a food box
    from the food bank is a new way to be.
I don't like this new norm; I don't seem to be adjusting well.
Four more years of this and we will be wishing for hell.
Or maybe we are already there.
The new norm isn't working and no one seems to care.
Society is changing there is a new face.
It is called the new norm and we are all caught in the race.
Our leaders don't seem to see that the new norm is not working, at
    least for the poor.
Good God, are we doomed to serve a sentence of misery with four more?
Whatever happened to prosperity when we all had a job?
When you paid your bill and made a living without being forced to rob.
There will always be greed, there will always be theft.
But after I cash my check, pay what bills I can there is no money left.
But I'm a back hills hillbilly, red neck son of a bitch.
I'll keep paying my taxes and feeding the rich.

The Day After Pill Something Went Bump

The night has passed a new day is born.
There were no bad dreams of past lovers scorned.
The dogs are acting strangely this morning something must have
    gone bump in the night
To cause such behavior and so much fright.
Nothing seem unusual to me, but I don't have a sixth sense of things
    I can't see
Of strange events of the past or strange things that will be.
The dogs are afraid of something I don't know what is there.
They won't leave the house like they usually do without a care.
The security alarm has been triggered it can't be easily reset.
It will just take some time for those dogs to forget.
I've checked around the house everything seems to be fine;
Nothing is missing or out of line.
I guess it's okay to leave the house now, I can't be afraid of the things
    I cannot see;
Of ghosts or goblins of things to be.
I don't know what it was that went bump in the night
To cause such terror and to cause such fright.
The alarm is reactivated; I'll see what this night shall bring.
I hope everything stays normal and no visits from a bump in the
    night or some strange thing.

This Pill or That

I lie in my bed and try to sleep.
Pain won't allow it at this time no matter how many sheep.
It really isn't much fun this thing they call age.
Another chapter of life, at the turn of a page.
Take this pill for that and that pill for this
And that pill over there will help me to piss.
Right now I lay here waiting for that pill to kick in, so I don't hurt
   anymore.
So I can have a good night of slumber and maybe even snore.
I'm dependent on the pharmacy for some quality of life.
As I fill like a guinea pig, I test another pill.
Its round and round each day with constant pain and strife.
Oh that pill is starting to kick in now. I'm starting to feel less pain.
Twenty more minutes I'll be in la la land, as outside the house its
   beginning to rain.
It's off to la la land now as my eyes are getting weary.
I hope I have pleasant dreams now and none that are scary.
Nighty night to all, I'm off to another place
That, that pill over there takes me to as I'm caught in this race.
Good night to all as I turn out the light.
To dream pleasant dreams of tomorrow and hope for less pain in my
   sights.
Nighty night, thanks for that pill over there.

Fan the Flames of Desire

If someone has talent don't throw water on the flames.

Continue to build the fire, encourage their desires, dint find fault or blame.

God shows us how he can work through us all if you give them a chance.

With a poem of words, a picture or a painting, you must take a stance.

To help and show others of how God chose you to do his work.

With the talents he gave you to help or give some form of encouragement to someone who might otherwise seem like a jerk.

Keep building your skills, hone them like a knife.

Keep building those talents for others to see God's inspiration he has given for you to share with others by your life.

Encourage a dream, encourage a goal, continue to fan the fire and see how it grows.

You don't have to be an eloquent speaker to share the message of God or his love.

You are a chosen vessel handpicked by him to be an apostle through your talents he has given you from above.

So build upon what you have been given to spread the gospel of why his son was risen.

Show your love through your art or your many talents with a passion like cloven tongues of fire.

Keep feeding the flames and building the desire.

When you teach another, you teach yourself.

Don't hide that talent anymore; take it down off that shelf.

Show others what you can do when you get inspired and see things in a different light and forget what you thought was you when you were tweaking and you were wired. That inspiration comes from another source that you really don't want to know.

And if you did at all you should tell this loser where to go.

He no longer has you numbered on a waiting list to take a number
and wait.
This loser won't take you anywhere you want to go to. He will keep
you from the pearly gates.
Remember you're the vessel that holds his spirit. Let God work his
miracles through you.
Let him work his mighty works in everything you do.

Thief in the Dark Stole Something of Yours

Have you ever met any people in your life, disgusting, vial, angry,
   ugly, of which you want nothing to do?
Or maybe bi-polar, possessed or just plain mean waiting to destroy
   either me or you.
Yes, I have come across a few in my life that don't know what it
   means to be good or kind.
But the worst of them all is when it is a family member and you want
   to kick them hard in the behind.
The behavior they show you or me is not of God's love for sure.
At least not of the true God that I love and worship; and you are left
   to find a cure.
We all have our good days and we all have our bad.
But when this behavior is present all the time in their lives and heart
   it makes you feel oh so sad.
You are left feeling hopeless and you don't know what to do to help, if
   you think you can.
But perhaps it's a fight you can't win because of the wickedness
   of man.
Some people have been fishing with an unforeseen source
And have been hooked into what they think is right.
But know nothing of the darkness that has a grip on them
Of which they show no light.
The only way to break this spell is to see the light above,
Accept God, and his son Jesus Christ into your heart and to know
   you are loved.
To walk then in your knowledge and power of God's will and lose the
   darkness that had you hooked.
And put the devil behind you now and know he no longer has you
   booked.
To do his evil, dark, disgusting plan because you never knew of his goal,
To leave you empty, sad and with no hope because he stole your soul.

Who Was This Man?

How will you remember me when my time has passed?
Did I give or leave you any memories of visions that will last?
Will you remember me for the good things I did
Or that grouchy old man. I am sorry I wasn't there at all when you
    were a kid.
I am here now, at least for a little while longer.
Will you remember me for the love I did give, to try to make you
    stronger?
Or will you remember the fights because you can only see things
    one way.
With the disrespect you gave me when I tried to make you stay.
Will you remember the talks we had that you never heard said
    that way?
Will you remember me at all with my hair of gray?
Will you remember the poems I wrote, the one that made you and
    others cry?
Will you remember me at all or possibly wonder why?
Will you remember when I tried to turn your life around and show
    you a better path to follow?
Will you remember me when I saw right through your pride of which I
    could not swallow?
Will you remember the struggles we shared of the cold of winter at
    my house?
Will you remember the rat you caught while trying to catch a mouse?
Will you remember me for the kind man and gentle man that loved
    his dogs till he dies?
Will these things mean anything at all will you even try?
Will you remember the rides we took with the dogs hanging out the
    doors?
Will you remember how we cut wood together and all the other
    chores?

I cannot say how I should be remembered that is not for me to pick
or choose.
Just try to remember me for who I was the things I did and why I
didn't take drugs or booze.
Your dad,
The Red Neck Poet

Angry Vial Man

You are a vial disgusting human being, like a rattlesnake ready to strike.

There is nothing good about your personality disorder and verbal abusive tongue that anyone does like.

You are angry with everything you say. You know all there is to know.

You show all the people you encounter by your angry tongue what you have to show.

You have nothing good to say or a positive thought to give.

You show everyone with your actions and your tongue exactly how you live.

My advice for you would be to see a priest as soon as you can.

Not for a confession, but to exercise those demons that control your soul, because you're a vial disgusting man.

I will call you Bullwinkle; you seem to be a-mister-know-it-all.

You view everyone as flying squirrels, flying around in circles until they fly into a wall.

You bring your problems with you to work. You are no pleasure to be around.

There is no good at all in that sole of yours, no, not any to be found.

So if you don't have a positive thought or anything kind to say;

Take those demons in your mind and find somewhere else to play.

Birthdays Suck

Happy birthday to me another year has passed.
The older you get, they come way too fast.
No special day for me, the boss called me in to work.
I can't refuse though I'd like to; he is such a jerk.
The kid made a cake and left it on the table with a card
And ran off to her friends to leave me alone with my dogs and a
    snowman in the yard.
Just another year older, how many more shall I endure?
It's no fun growing old and you're sick with no chance for a cure.
No special dinner, just a sandwich and a bowl of soup.
No one here to share the cake with, but the dogs, the kid flew the
    coup.
The cake was good though the dogs and I enjoyed it just fine.
Would have been nice though to share with some kin of mine.
So I'll go to bed now and think of birthdays past
And better memories of good times that will last.
60 years have come and gone; it seems in the blink of an eye.
With the things in between that often make you laugh and cry.
60 should be a special time; a mile stone in a man's life.
The down turn of all his accomplishments of his struggles and strife.
No special day for me I'll retire to my bed;
Think about tomorrow and did the dogs get fed?
Happy birthday to the Red Neck Poet. Turned 60 today.

Great Leaders Are Elected Not Born

Will the New Year bring prosperity to millions out of work?
While our turd leader flies to Hawaii to leave the country to pay the
bill.
With the title come the perks.
It sure seems odd to me though of all the missed days he calls in
sick.
Just to fly off to some resort in another land or place;
I think less and less of this leader; I think he's a dick.
I want to work… with little or no work to be had.
When you hear of another vacation this turd takes with his family, it
really makes me mad.
I think the fuel bill alone for one of those trips would easily pay my
mortgage for a year.
I hope this turd of a leader enjoys the warm beaches of Waikiki while
he's sipping on a beer.
Do you really think he gives a damn about you or me, while we
struggle to get by?
While he plots his next vacation destination on where next to fly.
Or perhaps what new pair of shoes that his wife will want to buy.
I didn't vote this time around; I liked neither of the above.
I see now it wouldn't have made any difference anyways, as the two
parties push and shove.
I no longer have any trust in our countries political views.
Come the next election I will enter my dog for the job,
At least you will have a better candidate on which to choose.
Our current turd of a leader sure can sing and dance.
He will offer you this and that with little or no hope and not as much
as a chance.
While millions of out of work people should rise up with their assault
rifles that will soon be banned and take a G-D- stance.

I see it all around the world, people crying for a change. I heard it
four years ago also, now how is that so strange.
This turd carries a good tune he sings of the same song from day
to day.
While the citizens of our once great land are given the check on
which they must pay.

Memories

The cold of winter is upon me now; I humble myself to my stove;
To provide me and my house with warmth and comfort now that I
am old and cold.
The glow of the fire warms my heart, as I reflect the memories past.
Now that I am old and things are way too fast.
It's good to slow down and sit back with a good book,
Throw another log on the fire and take a good look.
To a place off in the distance of a time long ago.
When people weren't so anxious and things were a little slow.
People helped each other and weren't quick to judge your faults.
It was a slower, kinder place with kids eating French fries at Frosty
Queen, along with shakes and malts.
To me, at least, it seemed easier with less stress and sorrow.
A place I like to go to, so I don't have to think about tomorrow.
I'll put another log on the fire to warm the chill and cold.
And remember the times of a child's past now that I am getting old.
A time of building forts and bang, you're dead; No, you missed me,
leaves memories of old chums and friends.
A time of long ago I wish they would have never end.
But with memories of times gone by with seasons and time as well;
Come wisdom, knowledge, temperance and patients.
We were young then and never knew the hardships that time does
bring.
To endure all of this, to grow old and reflect of times gone by with
the re-growth of each new spring.
I'll retire to my Easy chair and doze off to another place and time.
To remember and see old friends running and playing cops and
robbers and a time when you could buy more with a dime.

-Over Qualified-

Mr. Boss Man, you want all of my credentials and a live pulse upon a
  seat?
I must meet all of you requirements to be qualified for employment
  by your company of that I must meet.
Each year I have to get a physical and piss into a jar.
Look upon a chart to see if I am eligible and hope that my vision will
  allow me to see so far.
Then I get to be humiliated with a finger up my ass;
All so I can have a medical card to drive a truck for you. I sure hope
  again I pass.
I sure hope my resume suites you; I have worked 30 years to have my
  skills.
With all the tickets, fines and bullshit I have gone through to drive a
  damn truck it certainly has been no thrill.
To be a glorified delivery boy to get the load from point A to B.
To do it safely, responsibly and stay alive for another day.
Why and what the hell do you not see?
I drive this hundred thousand dollar piece of crap you call a truck to
  make you a better living than me.
With little or no respect from you, my boss, what is it you don't see.
I'll get up early and fight the wind and rain.
I'll drive the mountain passes in the winter and often have to chain.
Just to get your load there to make you and your company look
  good. While my body fights the pain.
Yes, this is my chosen career, boy did I mess up.
Looking back upon my years behind the wheel of a damn old truck.
I have made a humble living and tasted all the crap in between.
And done all the bullshit asked of me, why the hell have you not
  seen?
The only thing I have to look forward to is to die behind the wheel.
As I am jamming gears, pulling another pass or another hill.

My advice to you young man if you think of all the chrome and glitter
about this truck.
Don't think about it anymore. The boss makes all the money while
he throws you a couple of bucks.
Damn I hate driving a truck.

Spoiled Brat

When you want it your way all the time you will be disappointed more
    times than not.
It's not always about what you think you need, but what you
    already got.
You run off in a huff and a tantrum if things don't go exactly
    your way.
Like a five year old child, but that's not for me to say.
You show all the qualities of a brat! Spoiled, who was given all.
Your greed and your want, if you aren't awarded your beckoned call.
You should learn "need" from "want"; they are not at all the same.
How is God to answer your call to want, now who's to blame?
Be careful what you wish for. God works in very strange ways.
You ask for gold and glitter at the expense of others while someone
    else has to pay.
To God, time means little. He shows his riches to the ones deserved.
He doesn't hide it from you it is written in his word.
Ask and it shall be given, seek and you shall find.
God will answer your call on his terms. They are not always so kind.
God will try you as he did with Job and Lot.
He will put you through quite a bit of misery to see what you've got.
But he won't leave you stranded, he will reward you as he sees fit.
My advice for you, you spoiled brat, try to lose the attitudes if your
    choice and be grateful and humble for what you get.

Scary Story

As time flies by of your past; as the reflected memories seem to
   show;
Of a personal story book of your life, to leave for them to know.
From child to man, all the thing in between of lessons and things
   done and seen.
A story to be told of this person, like a movie upon a screen.
A history of events big and small to share with the ones that should
   know.
The story of a man's past of how this person lived his life and how he
   did grow.
From playing as a child in a playground swinging on a swing.
To chasing girls with a lizard or some other gross thing.
To a young man and discovering his first kiss.
To the broken hearts of all the other kisses in between.
Of a passage of a young man of the kisses that were missed.
The story is a long one that would take much too long to write.
This story has ugliness that I'm sure would fright.
It is a story you can fill in the missing blanks.
We will fast forward to a distant future of this man's life of when he
   fell into the ranks.
This man was sent to foreign land to fight to free another soil.
So that the ones back home could be free and safe to build their
   bank accounts as they labored and toiled.
It's not that great of a story, like most others that you see.
Nothing really to distinguish the reality of each other's life, nothing
   different from you or me.
Life went on and this man started a family.
It didn't seem to go the way it was meant to be.
They went their separate ways to bare the hurt and shame.
With years in between and children pointing fingers of who was to
   blame.

The hurt that is passed to others as their story unfolds
Of a time gone by as this man grows old.
He hopes that the hurt will stop one day. The scars will seal the
  wounds.
As he grows to see how his children raise their children he reflects of
  the past of a child running and laughing and of a child's sounds.

P.M.S. or Sybil

You are dynamite ready to explode.
You are unstable with your attitude always wanting to unload.
Your emotions have you walking on a tight rope swaying from side to
    side.
No thank you, I don't care to take this ride.
You are like nitro glycerin; it takes little to light your fuse.
Unstable, volatile, ready to explode. I will always step aside and watch
    the fireworks begin when you begin to let loose.
You seem to like the explosions with all the drama as you stir the mix
    together.
You like all the thunder and commotion and all the strong weather.
You can't seem to let things settle down and run a peaceful way.
You just keep stirring up the pot until you have your final say.
You think that you're entitled and you don't get your fair share.
You think no one cares about you or even has a care.
I don't know what else to do. I have spent a small fortune trying to
    help you get better.
I give up. The storm just keeps getting wetter.
I'll go to the poor house as you keep draining my bank account.
To try to help you with your volatile attitude and behavior of which
    there is no doubt.
Beam me up Scotty, I have had enough.
Living with multiple personality disorder is just too damn rough.

Tin Can House

I call it my house; it's really more of a can.
A place to escape all my worries, my dad's bitching and life's unjust
    plan.
It offers me solitude with the boredom that I must endure.
Because I now live in Shitville waiting for a cure.
It's not all that bad; I have made it my home;
An old Dodge motor home that I call my own.
Dad does his best to keep the rain off my head,
To pay the bills and keep me and his dogs fed.
When he is an asshole, I'll try to understand why.
I'll run off to my house and often I cry.
I think he tries to help what he can only see.
He really doesn't understand a lot about me.
So I'll run to my shelter where I feel safe and secure.
My tin can of a shelter of that I am sure.
I know he loves and cares about me and wants me to change,
But he is old and sick and at times very strange.
But he is my dad and wants for me the best.
I must prove to him and others as he puts me through his test.
My dad can be brutal at times I don't understand his ways.
I'll run to my tin can house when he rants and raves.
He tries to control his anger at me and tells me I must do the same,
That nothing gets accomplished with anger and blame.
So my house is more to me than just a place where I sleep.
It is my temple, my home of my things that I need and treasure that I
    keep.
I am grateful for what that old man has done,
Of what he shows and teaches me because there is nowhere left
    to run.
Dad's poem about me.

Tweekerville Nevada

Have you ever been to Tweekerville Nevada?

It's not much of a place to see.

White trash, middle class and Tweeker assholes those are one in three.

It is the largest White Trash Mobile Home Park, what a distinction to be called by.

But now, there is a new class of people, their called Tweekers that make their drugs to get high.

You will know one when you see them, they are usually skinny as a rail,

With Tweeker soars on their faces and they also look like hell.

They have that "death warmed over" look that makes you want to cry.

They will steal anything you have of value to sell, so they can get another high.

The ones that can afford to feed one will have a pit bull in their yard.

To keep people from getting to close to their meth labs. Try to spot them; it's really not that hard.

They think they have you fooled, but don't trust one for any chance.

They will steal you blind and leave you trying to hold up your pants.

So, if you're looking to buy some real estate to live in Tweekerville-

Before you buy that house you better invest in Iron bars upon your window seals.

And I hope you have a couple of guard dogs that will look and act the part.

To keep that Picasso painting hanging on your wall that some shit head in an art gallery calls art.

So welcome to Tweekerville Nevada; is it the retirement capitol that you dreamed?

I hope you like your new house and property before you too get creamed.

By some dumb assed Tweeker waiting for a score.

I hope you have a hand gun or a shotgun propped up beside your door.

I guess by now you can see and tell I have no like for a Tweeker.

You see I have a family member serving time behind bars because of a Tweeker lifestyle they thought was sweeter.

Bad Connection

When your down and feel like you're about to lose it all;
When you feel empty with your back against a wall.
When life has dealt you a bad hand; when people don't seem to care
 at all.
I reach out to my God and make another call.
It seems the line is disconnected and you are talking to yourself.
You wish he would answer you back, as you trudge along with your
 problems, as you put them on a shelf.
You hope to receive that call back and your father will make things
 go away.
You think the line is disconnected and you don't know what else
 to say.
You hope your God is listening you have no real understanding of
 how God will answer you back.
The understanding of his great power; the wisdom you seem to lack.
How do you talk to me my God? I would like to know.
Is it that nagging sixth sense? Is it the way you show?
I know not of your great plan as I stand here on this hill.
Teach me of the things I must do and see; as I try to do your will.
Talk to me God; the line seems to be only one way.
The transmitter seems to work but the receiver seems to be broken
 or you don't know what to say.
How must I hear you? Do you really hear my call?
Or am I to face my problems alone with my back against a wall?
Is it the still small voice that sometimes seems to tell me yes or no in
 the back of my mind?
Is that how you answer my call for help? I don't find that all so kind.
You leave me to make my own decisions of life. I don't seem to be
 doing very well.
Please answer my call for help; somehow show me how to tell.
I know you have spoken to others; your word, the bible tells me so.

Call me back, my God; I really would like to know.
There seems to a bad connection in the line I can't hear anything on
your end.
Please call me back my god; it is on you that I depend.
Waiting for your call…

Evil Man

Do you really think your better than this man or that?
What makes you so damn special? Is it your title or that hat?
Is it the money you make that put you in such a nice car?
Is it that nice suit you wear that tells the world who you are?
Did you step on others to get where you're at?
Was it your greed and lust for money that has made you so
    damn fat?
It is not the substance of a man that acquires wealth and fame.
But the substance of his heart of when he has no shame.
This man wears his pride for the entire world to see.
This man is the one who will tread on others including you and me.
To get himself to where he thinks he should be in this world of lust
    and greed.
To crush the spirit of the common man fighting for a need.
This man will wear a cloak of evil and put on the Darth Vader hat;
To crush and kill the good in man to show off his kingdom of where
    he is at.
I wear another costume it is called the armor of God.
I hold true to the staff of justice like an iron rod.
I fight the spiritual battle with the word of God in my hand.
Knowing that my rewards for my fight will come later in a different
    kingdom in a different land.
You evil bastard, you show me what you have to give.
No, not really, never mind! I already see how you live.

Seed of a Brand

As I leave my mark and legacy for my kids to see of my life.
The things I leave for them to show of my struggles and my strife.
A signature at the end of a poem, my brand upon a stick or a chair,
The things I would like them to know the most,
Is how much I love them and how much I care.
The things I can do are not for me, although I must fight to stay
    alive.
I do these things I do for you with love so you will learn how to
    survive.
When you teach someone else, you teach yourself. You perfect and
    hone your skills.
But the most important lesson is your passing on your knowledge
    and your legacy for your seed to flourish and see at their given
    will.
You will fight this fight of life; you too will leave your mark and
    signature to be seen and to be heard.
Never forget to teach your seed of God's knowledge, his love and his
    word.
Never forget where you came from, the apple doesn't fall far from the
    tree.
Live and teach yourself and your children
The things you must pass down for our future generation to see.
Know too your mark is being recorded by your God in his book of life
    for his kingdom to be.
Love Dad and your Heavenly Father Always,
The Red Neck Poet

The Cake is not so Sweet

I write poetry of life's situations of what I observe and see.
Sometimes they are humorous, but always with a message how life is
real and
Sometimes, ought not to be.
Throw something in the pot to screw things up; and you changed
the mix. Like a recipe certain things and ingredients must be
adhered to and followed.
When the mix of the recipe is broken or not done correctly, the cake
of life might be hard to swallow.
Follow the recipe and follow the rules.
Look at your life and see all the clues.
Is it going smoothly or somewhere did something go wrong?
Is there hope for a new ingredient to an old family recipe or the same
ol' crappy song?
If something needs fixing there is usually some kind of sign.
Did the cake not taste so sweet, or was it thrown out for the swine?
Add a little more sugar and spice to the mix next time you make the
cake.
Forget the sour apples that no one can take.
Vinegar and pepper are not the right ingredients for their recipe;
Try a little more sugar and honey in the mix of life and perhaps we
shall see.

Life

As I approach the last chapter of my life I reflect of life's lessons I
   have learned.
Of things I have won and lost and the money I have earned.
It has never been an ambition or a dream of mine to acquire wealth
   and fame.
I have little to show of my life's accomplishments, with no one else to
   blame.
I have lived my life with morals, a sense of right from wrong
To treat others with respect as it is warranted and do others no harm.
I have tried to balance the good from bad and see the lessons
   learned.
Of how I have lived my life and hoping that I won't get burned.
I hope the good out balances the bad and God holds a place for me.
The only way to know is when I leave this life and then in the next
   one then I'll see.
I have little to leave my loved ones of a sick worn out old man.
I keep writing these poems and letters for a message to be told
   between the lines or written in the sand.
I have suffered much and shed many tears throughout my life's span.
I have cried out to my God many times just wanting to squeeze his
   hand.
I have traveled this country and seen much through a windshield of a
   truck.
There is much to see of its beauty, and many times I have been left
   to wonder of God's power and I have been left awe struck.
I have served my country also and been sent to foreign lands.
I have walked the shores and beaches and felt the beaches sand.
What a mighty God it took to create such beauty to behold.
I love the beauty of his mighty hands that I have seen and touched
   now that I am getting old.

Enjoy the things of God's beauty while you're young. You might not
appreciate them until you get old.
Then you can tell stories to your grandchildren around a campfire as
they warm their hands from the cold.

Trinkets to be Shown

I have nothing of value to leave you when my life is done.
Very little to show for a lifetime of hard work and toil of life's
  battles won.
What I leave you I hope you will cherish and pass down to your own.
Nothing of real value. How do you put a price tag on something you
  hang on the wall to be shown?
A few things I have made from wood or metal. People say they are
  nice.
I leave them to my kids without a price.
You know not the value of an heirloom, there is no price tag.
They can't be replaced. Accept that they are what I have to give you
  of a life fought hard, there is no real value, so just be glad.
They are not to be sold.
They tell a story of a man's life. To be passed to each generation with
  a story told.
Family needs to know of their heritage, of how they came to be
  known.
So I leave you with these trinkets of my life to show future
  generations
Of a man's skills and crafts he taught himself; they were never
  shown.
Enjoy the art; develop these skills and talents of your own.
So you too can pass something down for the next generation to be
  known.

Taking a Vacation – Are We There Yet?

With the economy on the brink of collapse,
Not many jobs to be had within my field to grasp.
Not many to speak of, not many to be found.
I like my home and property. I don't want to be outward bound.
If that's what's next than I guess I must look in other places too.
There is certainly nothing here for me to have and nothing here
for you.
Our president doesn't seem to get it. Why should he if all his needs
are met?
While he's flying to his vacation destination in his private jet.
We all just went through four years of empty promises with this jerk
and now we get four more.
While he flies away on Air Force One with all his perks to a distant
shore.
It really amazes me that we don't have another civil war. I really don't
see the economy getting any better.
Recession my ass; check the statistics of the depression, no different
now from then; just a little wetter.
I got angry to think I fought in a war to give this ass the freedom to
fly where he wants to go.
That thousands have died for this jerk that has no birth certificate to
ever show.
All I keep hearing from this, our leader, is yes we can.
Well, I think he should pull his head out of his ass and be a leader for
our country and do a little more as a man.
What the hell has happened to our country? I would really like to
know.
People without a home and nowhere to go.
I just heard some homeless shelters won't even give you a meal
without a food stamp card.
What the hell is going on here? Should it be so damn hard?

Our government wants to control it all, especially you and me.
I hope there will be a better future for my children and grandchildren to see.
I am stuck here I have a mortgage that must be paid.
I love my house and property and the trees I have that provide some shade.
I am struggling to hang on while so many have walked away.
Where did they go? I really cannot say.
To a promised land of cupcakes and chocolate and change that was promised four years ago.
You have reigned Mr. President, what really did you have to show.
Really four more years of pain and sorrow.
What do you have to help the struggling people each day with no clear plan for tomorrow?
Thanks for nothing Mr. President. This is an epic time that history will tell.
Of how our leaders couldn't get anything done to help our people and our country.
We will see them burn in hell.

Bad Communicator

I went to pick up my check today and found out if there would be any
   future work.
I found out from the mechanic the boss is selling off most of the fleet
   of trucks he has. First news of this, what an ass and what a jerk!
Not so much of what he did, but not so much as a thanks for
   nothing call.
No talk to the crew or his employees, nothing at all.
Unemployment is started I don't know how long that will last.
With a mortgage, meds, a daughter to help get her life back and
   three dogs to feed, the money leaves the wallet and bank
   account way too fast.
I should trust my instincts better when you feel and know something
   isn't right.
I felt something was different with this man who would be my boss;
   perhaps he wears his pants too tight.
I think of all the years I have tried to listen to that voice inside my
   head,
The one that tries to tell me to stay away from this place all together,
   don't be deceived or fooled by what you hear and don't be
   misled.
I would probably be in a better place and point in my career;
If I listened a little closer to the whisper in my ear.
Pay attention people, there is always a snake oil salesman that will try
   to make you believe.
Don't put your life in the hands of any man that wants to trick you
   and deceive.
Walk away if it doesn't feel right. It's not a deal unless both parties
   can agree.
Listen to the whisper in your ear and perhaps in the future there will
   be something better for you to see.
It's too bad you can't test drive a new job; try it out for just a while.

Before you get locked in to something regretful, that ends with you
    face down in a pile.
You try to better yourself when you move on to another place.
Then you are stuck with no chance to return to what you left as you
    take a shit pie right to the face.
What do I do now God? Please whisper in my ear. I could use some
    words of encouragement so I don't feel like a loser to my family
    and loved ones, and not a total disgrace.
Will things balance out so I will have less stress and sorrow?
Will there be brighter days or a rainbow for tomorrow?
Whisper in my ear God and tell me what road I must follow.

Barbie Loses It

I see you bought a new car.
Does it show off your ego or define who you really are?
Do you like living the American dream?
Way over your head in debt, but living the good life to the limit with
    all of the extremes.
Plenty of plastic to cover all the bills and the debt.
With the bill collectors calling, "Have you paid this bill yet"?
Are you overdrawn at the bank? Did you really think that check would
    clear?
As you let your looks get you through your life grinning from ear
    to ear.
You have it all, but you own nothing. It took the collectors some time
    to figure your credit out.
The only free ride you have now is with a police man, as you huff and
    you pout.
Now the creditors are all claiming theirs from your estate.
And with them come the I.R.S.; they can't seem to wait.
Everyone is lined up all the way to the front gate.
Wanting to be paid, but it is too late.
What a grand ride you had. You played the part so well.
Of a fairy tailed aristocrat princess that has nothing left to tell.

Bad Habits Won't Change What's Wrong

Your prisons are the memories of the past that you see that you can't
   let go.
The ones that have molded your personality into what you do and
   show.
We all have our pasts; something's are better left behind.
Move on and learn from them, don't hit the remote for rewind.
Leave it there. Don't be imprisoned by what you know won't change.
You have seen this and done that, learn from it. Do something
   different, it shouldn't feel so strange.
No man knows the future or has a crystal ball to tell of coming
   events that will follow.
Learn from the mistakes you have made; is the pill really hard to
   swallow?
Don't keep doing the wrong thing time and time again.
You will be the loser all over one more time and you will never win.
Look closely at the patterns of your habits. It should be an easy road
   to take.
A roadmap to hell with every new mistake.
Take a different path. It might be the one that will change your life.
You will never know if you don't lose the anger built up in you.
Take the new road with less trouble and strife.

Mr. Clean

Blessed are they that have not seen yet believe. Spoken words in
time – by Christ our lord.
How do you believe in what you cannot see of a power to part the
Red Sea for the Hebrew slaves to Foard?
You showed your power God in sacred times of past.
Now I live in present times and wonder how much longer we can last.
With all the wrong in this world I often wonder why.
I raise my head up and yell my voice to you up there within the sky.
With all your power to create the heavens and the earth.
To put us here to be fruitful and to prosper for all that it is worth.
I see and hear of all the things going wrong here, God on what you
gave for us to use.
When will you fix it all? My God, it is not for me to choose.
I find it hard at times to worship what I cannot see.
To put my faith, in your son and my savior, for all that it should be.
To believe the words that were spoken by holy men as you worked
within their hearts.
God, I am a simple man and really not that smart.
Yes, I have read those words that were written so long ago.
For simple men and simple minds that we all should know.
With things unseen and things unknown of your powers to be shown
when you are ready.
For me to remain steadfast and await your call, stay calm and steady.
God, I await that day of your sons return.
For us, the ones that believe, but did not see, and of what all
mankind had the chance to learn.
Please God, clean up the mess.

Planting a Seed

I have taught myself many things in life, because I have had to do
things on my own.

When I grew up in the 60's throughout the rest of my life no mentor
taught me with instruction never shown.

You learn by doing; it's a process of touch and go and trial and error
and in the end we hope to know.

This thing called life takes many directions it has many roads to
follow.

With the up's and downs in between and the medicine at times hard
to swallow.

The issues we face build wisdom, knowledge and character; we learn
how to cope with emotions as well.

All the things God has to show us of his word of a future paradise; so
we as Christians don't burn in hell.

The joys of pleasures, the agony and the pain.

The things that teach us not to lie or steal and not to make the same
mistake time and time again.

The pleasures and pain that come with building a family and
watching the seeds of life grow on their own too.

The simple things of learning to dress one's self, to read and count
and to tie your shoe

Life seems long, but really it is quite short. With a story of each to tell
of how we process the things we see and do.

So if you have the chance to teach another to ease their journey, the
pleasure will come back to you.

The joy of seeing your seed grow also as you have given all you had
to give to them and that it came from your heart.

So your seed can have a better life and have a better start.

So they can follow the process to teach the seed of their own as well.

To watch that seed into what you as a parent hope they will become
with their own stories to tell as well.

Pull Another Hill

Is there any reason for any agony I have to endure?
For the diseases that I cope with because there is no cure?
To drive this truck and try to stay awake;
Because there is no prescription for me to take.
I am afraid that soon I'll be forced to quit my job because I pose a
    risk;
To myself and others because I am very sick.
Hopefully I can get some disability; it won't at all pay the bills.
For all the years I spent behind a windshield, jamming gears and
    pulling hills.
There won't be much money I'll live a meager life.
Just me and my dogs no more mortgage, no kids or a wife.
I'll be forced to sell the house, buy a motor home to live in; move
    somewhere close to the border.
So I'll be able to afford my meds and live out the rest of my life and
    get my effects in order.
For now I'll abide my time and stay alive to take another pill.
As I watch my life pass me by in the southbound lane while I jam
    another gear and pull another hill.

Stressed Out Dad

Am I your "Daddy Deep Pockets" to pay all your responsibilities and
    your bills so you can go on your way?
As I watch my bank account plummet without a thing to say?
You are all grown up now. Do you not see who you are?
I see you falling into your old habits, can't you see that far?
As long as someone else pays the bills, you think you can do as you
    please.
And all you think you can do is shake your butt, flutter your eyes and
    tease.
I'm sure the flavor of the month will gladly help you out;
As you unload all of your current issues as you scream and pout.
You scream and shout "Life just isn't fair!"
No its not, but have you ever been responsible for your actions
or took a close look at yourself if you dare?
You are young, why is there no perseverance or drive to succeed?
Is it too late or is there no longer any need?
There will always be a pain and some kind of sorrow.
Do you have any kind of plan for tomorrow?
Will you use your vices for some kind of excuse for your behavior?
Or trust in your Lord and in your savior.
What will you use to make the pain of life go away?
When you are old and wrinkled and have a head of gray.
There is no easy solution to mix up in a bowl or a pot.
Life has its ups and downs to show you what you have got.
Be grateful for what you have. Don't throw it all away.
There will always be a tomorrow and another day.

Soul Worthy

Every man's life has a story to tell.
Have you tried to live a good life or are you bound for hell?
How will you be remembered for the life you lived from birth to
    death?
When your life is over and you have taken your last breath.
Then the book of life is opened and it is turned to your page;
Will you humble yourself and thank God or show your anger and
    your rage.
Will your page tell a story of how you served your brother and done
    good?
Did you live your life for God and the best you could?
As the pages unfold your life's story is told;
From the day you were born to the day you are old
When your soul approaches those gates for your awards to receive;
Will St. Peter welcome you in or ask you to leave?
Will the lord accept your soul or will he boot you out?
Will the devil accept you in his kingdom as you scream and shout?
As you live your life while you're here on earth;
Will the pages tell a story of the substance of your worth?

30 Years

It's too late for me to be your father; I don't know where to start.
Thirty plus years of absence is no way to heal the broken heart.
To each we have suffered; to each we have shed many tears.
Thirty plus years of absence is way too many years.
To try to correct the wrong that has been done; to try to heal the
wounds of time gone by.
With the passage of time that has made us who we are; there is little
I can do no matter how hard I try.
We are miles apart on everything; we don't have much in common
at all.
The only thing I think I can say we share the same blood that run
through our veins, so the motor will not stall.
You are like your mother; cold hearted to the bone.
Who wants someone to take all the problems away when they are
yours, all your own?
The messes we create in time take years to clean and heal.
You must get started now; it will be a very steep and rugged hill.
You must have a plan and chip away at what you can lose.
It is all about choices. You must quit the drugs and booze.
To stay clean and sober will be a lifetime of commitment and
change.
You must fight the fight of life; no matter how hard or strange.

Dad's an Ass

How do you win the love of your children without showing favor to
   one or the other?

With each one's own personality being different as night and day it
   must have come from their mother.

Yes, I see the traits of myself in each of them, but I would like to
   remain on neutral ground.

To love one above the other is absurd. They will know this someday
   when I'm no longer around.

The rivalry between the two of them is intense and has divided most
   all of the family and put most in their worst behavior.

I think at times that the only cure for their bickering and fighting will
   be the return of our Lord and Savior.

For me the dad I'm caught in the middle with no easy plan of what
   to do.

I help one, I lose the other. I wish they could see things through my
   eyes, wear my hat or wear my shoes.

Most of the time I'm an asshole or a jerk with a credit card or a debit
   card.

Just trying to pay the bills, with my own life to live when times are
   very hard.

I don't seem to say or do the right thing. I suppose that is just the
   way I'm wired.

I wish I didn't have to work anymore and I could all together be
   retired.

But for now I'll have to work a little longer and fight off the hurt and
   pain.

Keep hoping I do and say the right thing with my offspring and see a
   rainbow through the rain.

I love both my daughters; good, bad or indifferent, regardless of their
   faults or their deeds.

Like god, he loves his children also and like me he will provide for
    their needs.
I think in life we pick and choose who and how we love.
The circumstances of our live teach us how to push and shove.
But as a dad or a father we won't always get things right.
You as offspring must learn to turn the other cheek and forgive also if
    you might.
So as a dad or a father, remember if you can;
I am not Jesus Christ, I am just a man.

Prayer for a Child

I pray my God that you heal my child and relieve me of my pain.
Restore her mind back to her before her addictions consumed her
    and robbed her of her brain.
The lies, the deceit and her evil heart hurt me every day.
Because of the lifetime of addictive behavior and abuse; now I get
    abused for trying to save her life.
I was not the one led astray.
She chose to live the black life as a street punk on the street.
She learned how to survive in the city of sin; a beautiful young
    woman once the girl you'd love to meet.
Then the thief in the night stole that child and made her now what
    you see.
A confused burnt out addict that seems to know all the answers as
    long as they don't affect the reality of who she used to be.
That life is gone from her; I pray that you would bring it back.
I try my best as a father to help this angry child of mine while I watch
    her world turn black.
I see the repeated mistakes she makes; with no corrective plan in
    mind.
She runs and hides from her obligations of any form or kind.
The family has turned their backs on her, I can truly understand
    now why.
To change your life you must want to help yourself, at least give it
    a try.
I tell her of her behavior how she must recognize her anger that
    consumes her heart.
But for me, I'm an ass of a dad to help her make a new start.
She is a user and a taker; to take everything and more;
And leave you to heal your broken heart as she slams another door.
Dear God, I am at my wits end. I don't believe there is much more I
    can take;

Before I too am forced to turn my back. A decision I do not want to
make.
This child of mine must learn to lose the anger. I believe I try more
than I should.
I'm not the evil mean nasty man she perceives me as I really am
trying to see the good.
Please my God teach her to learn from her past,
Because I hope that her anger and bad attitude somehow will not
last.

Electronic World

We live in an electronic instantaneous world where everything is as
easy as a touch.

We have created a society of pussies. I don't care for it that much.

Our children think they must have everything and they must have
it now.

I think that most would believe that milk came from a jug and not
a cow.

The things we have and the things we use; to me my mind seems
hazy.

As I see and watch this generation of youth become more and more
lazy.

Games for this and games for that all controlled with a button and a
stick.

As I watch and see our youth disintegrate before my eyes it makes
me feel quite sick.

Do you have nothing better to do than have your time consumed by
a computer or a game?

Am I old and behind the times and wonder who's to blame?

This country was founded on determination, strong will and a back.

Too bad this generation of youth has no back bone on that they
seem to lack.

I sit and ponder the fate of our own country. As I separate the calves
from the herd.

I wonder what will become of it when I am gone and it is run by a
computer geek or a nerd.

Sticky Fingers

You have sticky fingers, your fingers stick like glue.
Not because you haven't washed them, this just seems to be a part
of you.
You can't seem to put things down that do not belong to you.
You have sticky fingers that attach themselves like glue.
Sticky fingers like the glitz and glitter and things of any worth.
I don't recall them being sticky when you were naked at your birth.
I guess the pals you choose to hang with helped to pour the honey
on your hands.
That you have never been able to lick away because you chose not to
take a stand.
Your reliability and reputation are renown with all your clan.
You have sticky fingers that have been the demise of many of man.
You may gain your credibility or perhaps your fifteen minutes of
fame.
With a rap sheet a mile long, then who will you blame.
I think you should find a stronger soap to wash the glue off of those
fingers;
And tell those spirits in your mind they no longer have a place left to
linger.

The Sacrificial Lamb

Is there any shame for the money that you take?
For the lifestyle you did choose and for all of your mistakes.
The world has taught you plenty of how not to live your life.
It's time to break the co-dependency upon others; be it wrong or be
    it right.
Now I am old and in my golden years.
Am I to use my money to wipe away those tears?
The entitlement you fill is yours does not justify the sacrifices I have
    made to keep you free.
Do I have to suffer all your anger until you finally see.
Is there a reason why you think that what is mine is yours as well?
Please tell me because it's not for you to sell.
You say you want your life back. You have said this many times
    before.
As you run off with your flavor of the month to find another score.
I have seen and learned also the lifestyle of a Tweeker.
Now I am in my golden years I cannot work as I once did because
    now my body is much weaker.
I should be able to enjoy the fruits of my labor to spend and have as
    I see fit.
Before I am dead and buried and no one gives a shit.

The Common Man

Some people say that I am cold and harsh with things I say and do.
The reality of life is hard and brutal at times you will learn this before
　your time is through.
The path we take the road we choose is not always what we think.
You must work to fulfill your dreams, raise a family, and have a home
And if you are lucky enough in a tough world where jobs are hard to
　come by and the economy does stink.
Prices of commodities keep rising and the pay stays the same.
The greed of man has shown his plan; it's all profit, wealth and gain.
Everyone has their hand out; wanting their slice of pie.
Some will take a bigger slice than you will get, it makes you
　wonder why.
So choose the road you take wisely; learn and do all you can.
Try to upset the balance and don't become a greedy man.
Work hard, but be thankful; live your life without shame.
Thank God for the blessings you have and know who really is to
　blame.

Bad Ass-it

I would like to see some return for the money spent to help change
    that bad ass-it attitude.
I have seen little for all the money that I have spent on you. Don't you
    at all find that kind of rude?
I fight with those demons in your mind to see that anything at all
    gets done around this place.
As you throw the poison from your mouth and make a hideous face.
You seem to have an answer for everything you seldom stop to see.
Could it be your bad ass- it attitude or quite possibly I'm blinded
    by those demons that control your mind to see it just might be
    about me?
The road you take is rocky with many twists and turns.
When will you see it just might be your bad ass-it attitude; when, if
    any, will you learn?
You are a bad ass-it. I see it in who you are and what you do.
You are a bad ass-it; hard core; through and through.
You are a bad ass-it; I think I'll leave you all alone.
You are a bad ass-it with a heart as cold as stone.
Your problems of life are attacking you from every side.
But you are a bad ass-it; will you fight or run to hide?
Do you think that all of your tattoos make you a bad ass-it? Do they
    make you tough?
Will you be a bad ass-it when life gets a little rough?
Does your bad ass-it attitude put you in a different class?
Does it separate you in the field of life or make you look like the ass?
Your anger and bad ass-it attitude and behavior have all running to
    take cover and to hide.
Not many want to be around a bad ass-it or walk with you by your
    side.

Super Jackass

You think you are so super at this or that.
I don't quite see it the same as you, but I do see where you're at.
You seem to have a high opinion of yourself,
as you put on that name tag and take that hat off the shelf.
Does that change your personality to be condescending and a bully
to treat people like crap?
Are you caught up in being that super person in your mind; are you
caught in that trap?
Do you think that climbing that ladder puts you in another class?
As your abusive and bullying tongue makes you look like a super ass.
Are you proud of your accomplishments at belittlement of another?
Because your title and authority allows you to beat up on your
brother.
Do you see yourself as esteemed and respected by all your peers?
I think you do not see yourself as others do.
Will you be a jackass throughout your remaining years?
You see super asses everywhere you go.
You know the ones that have nothing of substance within, but have
everything to all to show.

Repel It

I'm not much of a people person. I don't like people all that much.
Is it the times of man or am I out of touch?
Now don't get me wrong; I don't want to offend you with a finger or a
slap.
I just don't get it…that music you listen to that you think is rap.
I guess it is me. I am old now and think that it is just crap.
I use the electric wheelchair at the market to get a few things that I need.
I am regarded as a piece of shit as you pay no heed.
People in a hurry to get what they need off of a shelf.
Maybe that's why I don't like people, because all they think of is their self.
Oh, there's a cow in the isle that won't move her cart.
So I'll maneuver my electric wheelchair as close as I can and release
my gastric fart.
As the vapor arises and the labels peel from the cans; I can then
stroll the isles with ease.
Watch out for that old man in his electric cart because he doesn't
play games or tease.
He has a dying liver that will release a foul old man's fart at will.
As you see him strolling down the aisles in his electric cart, as he
takes another Carter's liver pill.
He needs a second income. You can get his services online.
You need something cleared right away; call him any time.
Want to clear a line into a club or your favorite place to eat?
Cal the Electric Fart in a wheelchair; he will for a fee gladly get you a seat.
His farts can peal paint from a wall if you need to repaint a room or a
house.
Or perhaps you want a day alone to do your own thing away from
your significant other; perhaps it's your spouse.
You name it…He can clear it or repel it, even put curls in your hair.
Call the old fart in his electric shopping cart and his motorized chair.
Call 1-800-Repel It.

The Tornadoes Vortex

You live by your senses instead of the spirit of God within.

You allow Satan to control your mind and actions as you are caught in the vortex and turbulence of the tornadoes evil spine.

He is subtle. He will suck you into the evil mix.

He will teach you of his pleasures and teach you of his tricks.

Like candy to a baby, he will give you every desire.

As you are pleasured by your senses and taught by the master who is the great liar.

He has been hear from the beginning and has had time a plenty to perfect his skills.

You are just a puppet dancing to the master as he moves in for the kill.

He cares nothing of the shell that is the outward appearance of the soul of man.

His goal is to kill that spirit of God and Christ within you, if you abide by his plan.

You seem to do well at accepting all his bribes, as he darkens your heart to what is true and pure.

As the master builder shapes and molds your mind to do his evil plan and hopes you won't find the cure.

What will it take for you to understand the master's evil plan?

He is the master builder shaping you by your senses throughout your life's span.

There will be more tragedy and sorrow before he lets go of you.

How much will you take of his pleasures before his plan is through?

I hope for your sake that you can turn that spark in your heart into a raging fire.

Tell the master builder to go to hell, because he is the master liar.

Price Tag for a Soul

How would you put a price tag on a life you say you never had?
Finally having some form of family, it seems you would be somewhat
glad.
But with time comes all the dust that has been swept under the rug.
As the skeletons unveil themselves about your life and the things that
have made you who you are,
you can't hide or shrug.
You think I owe you. Would you like that price paid in full?
How are you to put a price tag on what I say is a lot of bull?
You are a psychopath, always blaming others for your mishaps and
issues that arise.
A liar and a thief that has no remorse for who you hurt or victimize.
You are quite good at what you do, you have perfected your craft and
skill.
You have sucked me dry for all I have, as you move in for the kill.
As you thrust the knife into my heart and I breathe my last breath.
I give you my dying wish before my final death.
I wish you could see the sorrow and fill the pain that comes with a
long lived life.
The loss of my children, my struggles and all of my strife.
To live my life in hurt and shame and a few shed tears.
Not knowing but caring throughout all of those years.
So as I take my last breath, consider the price paid in full...
For there is no price tag that can be put on a life of hurt and shame
of an old and worn out soul.
So as you go about your way with your prize that you hold dear.
Remember, as you go through your life there will be a price tag also
and you will shed many tears.

Lost Daddy's Girl

Being Daddy's girl, nothing could go wrong.

But when you left me, life was hard and long.

From the time I was three I had a hole in my heart.

I always wondered how long we would be apart.

Mom always told me "You will never see him." "He never wanted you anyway."

Deep down in the core of my soul I knew we would meet again someday.

My adolescent years go by and not a word said.

The hole in my heart is yearning for comfort as I try to ease the thoughts of wonder in my head.

The early teenage years were an awkward and difficult time for me.

Looking and acting different from everyone, all my friends and family.

Feeling alone and trapped in my own thoughts of "why me".

I just don't understand how you could have done this to me; I feel so ugly.

I'm 18 and have been on my own for quite a while now;

The independent life of working and partying like it's going out of style.

The drinking and drugs were the escape from it all.

I'm still asking myself is it what I'm looking for? Is this my beckoned call?

I met a wonderful man I think he is my soul mate.

We moved into an apartment together. I wish you were here to ask if this is my fate.

Oh my! Regardless, "Aunt Flow" hasn't made her monthly visit, I'm 2 weeks late!

Time flies by, a house and two children to be a role model for.

Now all I need is a ring on my finger; God only knows what he has in store.

I'm wearing a long white dress with a bouquet in my hand.
Who's going to walk me down the aisle to pass me on to that
handsome man?
I thought about you every day. I even found your address and
number.
I was encouraged not to call and thought to myself who am I to
encumber.
A couple of years go by and I'm outside watching my children play
and only wish it was the same for me.
I receive a phone call; who could this be?
A man on the other end telling me he is my father.
My first reaction was to hang up; why bother.
I hesitated and you said please don't hang up on me.
I have a liver disease and it's hereditary.
All of a sudden the hole in my heart felt filled.
You have been there all of these years; you have been there in spirit. I
was thrilled!
I still don't understand why now; why with this? Why not fight for your
kids?
As far as I'm concerned, most people in these situations would
forbid.
Don't get me wrong, I'm happy and feel complete now you're back in
my life.
I thank you for giving me the opportunity to know who you are and
relieve some of your strife.
I now know and understand what makes a child complete.
My children will not know of the pain and suffering of a heart left
incomplete.
The Red Neck Poet's Daughter
Amber L. Soto 2013

Always There

You went from child to adolescent without my hand of guidance in
    your life.
All the things in between then you became a wife.
I wasn't there but you have done just fine.
Although, you did not know, I was with you all the time.
I missed all those birthdays and wondered where and how you were.
Never really knowing but always with you, on that you can be sure.
Wondering how you have grown, of all the things you love and enjoy.
Your friends, your music, the things that make you sad and happy
    and that first kiss from that boy.
You have grown into a fine woman with a fine family of your own.
I was always there with you without you ever knowing.
The time, the years, they sped so fast by.
I know that you never knew and asked the question why.
It was never your fault. Life takes its twists and turns.
With it, it has given each of us plenty of opportunity to grow and
    learn.
Although never with you in the flesh, I was always there.
In your heart with my presence knowing you would always care.
I love you Amber.

Gene Pool

I was the swimmer that made it in this gene pool of life.

Out of the thousands of others, why me? I'm no one special. As I struggle with life issues as well as its strife.

I'm sure there were better swimmers much qualified than me.

I'm a dumb assed truck driver. I have no PHD.

Why did I break through the barrier? How and why did I make to that warm and cozy place?

To spend nine months within my mother's womb, then pop out with the agony upon her face.

Was that agony of pain or agony of joy?

As I proceeded out in the elements of life to begin my life's story.

The story of this swimmer has been long and been hard.

It hasn't always been cupcakes and jelly beans. I've struggled for every yard.

Why was I chosen out of thousands of others that tried and failed?

In this gene pool of life with my not so special story to tell.

Yes, I've had a full life. I've seen many amazing things.

I've added to the gene pool of life as well and as they have struggled to take flight without any wings.

Now they will have their lives with their stories to tell.

As the flourish and prosper and add to the gene pool of life as well.

Chasing a Vane

The life of a minor is hard and tough.

Drilling, blasting and mucking that ore every day.

Timbering those stops following the vain when you can see it for
    another day's pay.

You supplemented the pay check with a chunk of ore here and there.

Carried out in your lunch box hoping no one will catch you or even
    care.

You blast those holes and you fill those cars as you follow that elusive
    vain.

You go home with a massive headache from the dynamite and your
    body fills all the pain.

You lay another set to inch farther into the hole.

Into the bowels of hell you go wondering if the devil is waiting at the
    end of that set so he will steal your soul.

No, you made it safely to see the light of another day.

To do it again tomorrow as you drill, blast and lay another set in the
    bowels of hell, as you earn your pay.

You did this all your life then the Lord carried your spirit away.

Where the streets are paved with gold that you didn't have to dig,
    blast or chase that elusive vain to earn your pay.

Now you get to enjoy all the rewards the Lord has to offer and look
    down on the ones you worked so hard for.

Like the one that wrote this poem for you dad.

As he waits to see you some day and walk those streets of gold with
    you and watch the sun set upon those golden shores.

To my dad who worked in those mines all his life for his family.

I love and miss you

Your son, The Red Neck Poet.

Pawn Shops

The pawn shops all love you. They know you by your name.
When they see you walk into the store to pawn an heirloom that was
    given to you to pass down. Now isn't that a shame?
Do you have anything remaining that was given to you as that pawn
    shop owner throws you a couple of bucks and you walk out the
    door?
Knowing he will make a profit when he sales that priceless heirloom
    that is gone now for sure.
Nothing to pass down to a loved one to tell the story of the past.
Pawned to a pawnshop for a high that did not last.
Nothing to be saved for a future generation to see or enjoy.
Because you had to satisfy that craving for another high, as you kill
    the past and watch as the heirloom gets destroyed.
Not just the heirlooms, but anything of value, so you could get a
    high.
As your children and your family hang their heads and cry.
The things you care about all fit into that shell you call a soul.
As you pawn another heirloom and you try to fill that hole.
The hole that is empty that burns within your heart.
Beckoning you to start all over fresh and make a new start.
But I don't see that day starting any time real soon.
As you walk into that pawn shop and pawn another family heirloom.

Slamming Door

"F" you dad is what you hear. I don't have to listen to you anymore.
As you hear the screams and yells and the slamming of the door.
You're hurt and saddened as this child tries to even up the score.
As she walks away one more time with the slamming of the door.
You've seen and heard it many times this child has all the answers it
    would seem.
You're an ass and all in between as you hear those angry screams.
You wonder what should I have said, could I have done some more?
As the child curses you and walks out that slamming door.
Go ahead and leave for now you think you know it all.
But let me tell you something, daddy is not always going to be there
    to open up that slammed door or pick you up off your ass.
After you have taken a nasty fall.
So go ahead and live your life and try to do it well.
As my house returns to normal and only time will tell.
It sure is quiet around here. No more screaming and yelling
    anymore.
No more cursing and no more slamming of the door.

Burning Bridges

You made it across that burning bridge as you glance back for one
more look.
How will you find your way back home now, after everything you
took?
You burnt that bridge right to the ground. Did you not think that it
was the only way back home?
What will you do and how will you live now that you are all alone?
You would think it would be cheaper and wiser to leave that bridge
intact.
To build that bridge of trust and respect will be so much harder now
with the way you choose to behave and act.
How can you blame another for how you choose to live?
It's always take what you want when you have nothing in your heart
to give.
That road back home will be a long one. Perhaps you won't be able
to build again the bridges mighty span.
Because I know of one you lied to, stole from and crushed his heart;
an honest working man.
What will it take? When will you see there are no more bridges to
burn?
When no one is there but yourself standing between the chasms;
because you refuse to learn.

Punk

What's so cool about your hat turned up and sideways and your
    pants down below your ass?
And that Japanese car that you think is so fast?
I guess I'm old and I just don't get it.
To me you look like a punk and a piece of shit.
And what's with all those tattoos and the jewelry hanging from your
    face?
Here, let me arrange it for you. It looks so out of place.
You wonder why you don't have a job, while you sleep till noon.
Then lie around watching videos or watch a stupid cartoon.
I don't know. I guess I'm old and don't like it all that much.
With this punk generation that thinks I'm out of touch.
What's that you say? You have an interview at Mickey D's today?
Good luck with that as they send you on your merry way.
Oh, you think you nailed it as you dressed for success.
Please tell me you got the job so I don't have to guess.

Boy Toy – Drunk Punk

Are you happy yet? Are you doing well?
You and your boyfriend in that flee bag motel.
Does he fill all your hearts desires? Does he hang on to your every
    word?
Or is he like all the other flavors of the month; just a loser turd.
Oh! He has a DUI, now isn't that just sweet?
And with your meager job! You are one kick from the street.
Oh! He likes his booze and drugs just the same as you.
What am I supposed to think as a parent? What am I to do?
Oh! You had a drunken fight now you are back in jail.
How would I have guessed it's just too hard for me to tell?
My phone is ringing; it's you on the other end.
Why is it me you always call? Isn't there anyone else you can depend?
Just another charge against you. You are already on parole.
When will you learn and see the picture? How much will you pay the
    toll?
Your one step closer to going back.
Please get your head out of your ass when it comes to your choice of
    men and your addictions the wisdom you sure lack.
Is this the future you envisioned? Do you have any goals in mind?
Just doing it day to day with your boy toy and life is not so kind.
Can't you see what you're doing? He is as screwed up as you.
How is he helping your addictions and your behavior? Again, as a
    parent there is nothing I can do.

Letter to an Addict

Did you get my money's worth now that you are free?
As you think and thought only of what you need and want and not a
  damn about me?
You have stolen and pawned what is not yours;
To satisfy your demons and that evil curse.
Things and money can be regained; what price have you paid?
As you surf the web for a man to hide your sorrows and to get laid.
Your addictions have cost me plenty. They have come with a mighty
  cost.
As your family suffers from it all of what they have lost.
Can you heal those broken hearts or the trust that has been taken
  away?
Because of your addictions and your lifestyle, because you have been
  led astray.
Do you think of who you hurt or affect when you steal that credit
  card?
As they struggle to pay your fines to keep you free, keep you clothed
  and a roof over your head when times are very hard.
You buy a smart phone with my card and think I won't find out
And when confronted, I'm an ass as you scream and shout.
What is wrong with you! You care not who you hurt.
As you use and victimize your family and treat them like a piece of
  dirt.
You think and act like nothing matters; rules and laws don't apply
  to you.
As you disregard any obligation as another victim of yours gets
  screwed.
You are a scavenger living from hand to mouth each day.
No thought for tomorrow, no goals or a plan that I see of changing,
  as you go about your merry way.
You will grow old someday as time takes its natural course.

Will you ever get your life together or victimize a different source.
Like your mother, you are one in the same.
Looking to score another bag as you play life's game.
She found her sugar daddy to take care of all those aches and pains.
You have allot to catch up to if you think there is much to gain.
I keep telling you to take the test drive before you park it at the gate.
But all you choose to drive are all those broken down Vegas because
you are impatient and choose not at all to wait.
Your disgruntled and broken hearted dad

The Excavator

You have dug that hole you call your life.
I hope you have it roped and braided so no one innocent shall fall
    within.
The life you think and say you want as the drama starts to spin.
The hole keeps getting deeper. How and when will you stop digging
    to climb out?
What will it finally take for you to realize; your vodka and drugs aren't
    what life's all about?
Perhaps you could throw the drugs and vodka bottles in that hole
    you dug and cover it to the top.
What and how far will your addictive behavior take you before you
    will see that you must stop?
They say that each must hit rock bottom.
Damn, haven't you dug that far yet? How much more will you lose
    before you see that you could have had it and your life was set?
Your booze and drugs won't comfort you once the high is gone.
Will you lover contribute to your abuse and have a shoulder for you
    to cry upon?
The sedatives will go away... like a gentle breeze within the night.
How much more digging can you endure before you finally get it
    right?

Left Holding the Bag

How are those demons behaving; the ones that seem to control your
mind?

The ones you can't seem to lose and the ones you can't seem to
leave behind.

Life is good when things are easy and seem to be going well.

It's when thing are not that those demons show themselves; and you
know their straight from hell.

That's when the demonic behavior changes you and you want a drink
or a toke.

When you partake with those demons your life turns into a joke.

You do stupid things and hang out with people you say are your
friends.

But where are they when the booze and drugs are gone and you are
the one left to defend.

You will be turning mid-life soon. Don't you think you should grow up
and start a better plan?

Will you wait until you are old and grey and then it's too late to
reclaim the innocence of youth?

You are left holding a bag of crap that reflects your life span.

Do you think you won't grow old? Perhaps not if you continue upon
this path.

But even simple calculations are against you. You just need to do the
math.

The odds are against you. The deck is not stacked in your favor.

It should be an easy choice to make; go to hell with those demons or
except your Lord and savior.

Quiet

He was a quiet kid, kind of shy and reserved.
Never saying much in a conversation, but hanging on to every word.
Always polite in his manners; not causing panic or alarm.
Quiet, gentle and hind to animals and never doing them any harm.
He has a special way with them. They know they are safe in his
    hands.
Comforting and caring for the sick or injured and obeying to his
    commands.
I watched this boy grow from a child to a young man.
Not always there, but caring and teaching him when I can.
I watched this boy graduate from school to start his life from scratch.
Like a fledging bird spreading its wings for the first time from the
    incubated hatch.
This boy's life will be long as he starts his new life from the nest.
There will be many challenges as he conquers life's mighty quests.
I know he will do well. He has the heart that will prevail.
As he sits around the table someday with stories he will tell.

Second Class Please!

I have been rode hard and put away wet.

Not in the embrace of some lovers passion.

But of a cruel and greedy thing called work; that you would like to forget.

We all must go through it; unless you are born with a silver spoon.

No, not me; not within my lifetime or of any time very soon.

I can tell you of that silver spoon class!

And where they ought to put that spoon. It's not their mouth; that's for sure. You can shove it up their ass.

They think and act like their better; when it comes to white trash like me.

I wish they can wear my boots or see through my eyes; then perhaps they would see.

They walk around ridged with that spoon stuck firmly up their ass.

They string you along with a meager pay check that you hope will provide you with a tank of gas.

For now I am thankful I have what their money will not buy.

A place reserved for me with my Lord in heaven; when I shall meet him in the sky.

That 15th Load

It is about time. It is about money; at least that is what I'm told.
As you push yourself and the truck to get that extra load.
It is money out of your wallet as you sit there waiting while the loader
   operator talks on his radio and scratches his ass.
Oh, and don't forget to slow down on the haul road and never pass.
There are so many things that can go wrong; you are dependent on
   that truck.
As you push the envelope a little harder and try to make a buck.
You jeopardize your pay check as you try to pay your bills.
Because you need that 15th load; because you already are living day
   to day without any thrills.
You pay what bills you can than go about your day.
And hope you get a phone call and a dispatch for tomorrow, so you
   can earn that 15th load for another day of pay.
If the crusher breaks, you are screwed, you have lost another load.
As all the trucks back up down the hill all the way back to the road.
Round and round you go in the pursuit of that elusive 15th load.
Because that's how you make any money here; at least that's what
   I've been told.

A Senior Moment

As I pause for a senior moment and go through the Rolodex within
my mind.
To remember some forgotten event or moment that age had taken,
because it's not so kind.
The wires start to short circuit, the smoke pours out my ears.
As I try to remember of that moment frozen in time that has been
robbed throughout the years.
It angers me at times and sure takes longer to remember of the
event.
Was it a pleasurable time; was it time well spent?
The good times are there just as well as the bad.
As you struggle through the Rolodex within your mind; trying not to
remember the sad.
How many memories can this devise between my ears hold?
The Rolodex that is my mind, now that I am having my senior
moments because I'm getting old.
I have been told I'm senile. Hell, what does that mean?
I'm just old and forgetful. The mind I once had is now not so keen.

New Cadillac...Road Trip

Do you feel special as you climb into that truck?
And the boss rolls by in his new Cadillac and throws you a couple of bucks.
You bust your ass. You do all the work.
While the boss drives by in his new Cadillac and enjoys all the perks.
You're lucky if you can pay the bills; yet alone buy a tank of gas to even get to work.
As you watch the bass roll by in his new Cadillac enjoying all the perks.
You wish you had some extra money just to get out of town for a while.
As you watch the boss roll by in his new Cadillac, doing it in style.
Yes, that truck is shiny, with all the whistles and bells.
But when the checks are delivered, that the story tells.
The story of who makes all the money...
But will that Cadillac make the trip with the boss or breakdown along the road?
When the trumpet is sounded for the ones the Lord has called to the land of milk and honey.

Revolving Door

Are you enjoying that new revolving door you had installed thinking
that it would bring you that perfect employee?

As your secretary hands you a new stack of job applications for you
to shuffle through and enjoy.

Did that new employee break a hidden rule? Is that why you let
him go?

Or was he not the one you really wanted or were looking for?

Now he hangs his head and leaves out that revolving door.

You tell your secretary to place an ad in the paper and on the net for
a new employee.

Because you didn't find anything or anyone in that stack of
applications you enjoyed.

You wonder isn't there anyone qualified to take the same crap we
have to offer as before.

As you glance over at your secretary and see her laughing and rolling
on the floor.

Because she knows that as soon as you think you have found that
perfect employee, she will see him or her leaving through that
revolving door. There will always be a new face or a pulse upon a
seat.

But will they have the experience and qualifications that you will pay
for that you desire and seek.

The Apprentice

What's your name? Hands down, you seem to be the finest from
what I hear and see. Will you be my mentor?

So I can be a turd also and get flushed down the toilet of life along
with you. Because, like an addict, you didn't find the cure.

Boy, you're the Mr. know it all. Will you teach me all you know? Come
on now, is that all you have to show?

You can do better if you please.

Don't keep me hanging on. Teach me how to be a turd, don't play
with me or tease.

What's that you say? I didn't quite catch that crap spewing out of your
mouth as you shower me with spit in my face.

Please slow down while I wipe this crap up of its intended place.

Damn you're good. Please teach me all your tricks.

So I can learn how to be a turd like you. The one who is a prick.

All I have to do is watch and listen to the finest turd in town. Gee
master, I'm happy for what you have to show.

I never have to read your mind you are always glad to let me know.

Thank you for letting me be your apprentice. I have been lucky to
learn from the best turd I know.

Tin Man

Did Dorothy not lube you? She left you in the rain.
Is that why you're so rigid when you move and you feel the pain?
You're walking so rigid like your rusted up and can't move so well.
Did Dorothy not lube you last night? I know she won't tell.
Did she miss a few joints? Is that why you're so stiff?
Did she have a date with the scarecrow and that's why you're so
    pissed?
Any way you look at it, you are stiff as a nail.
Did Dorothy not lube you? She will never tell.
Maybe it's that broom that the scarecrow shoved up your ass.
No one will tell of the story of that fair lass.
Maybe you can get the wizard to help you pull that broom from its
    solid place.
And you wouldn't be so rigid and we would see a smile upon your
    face.
Or perhaps Dorothy could look at her date book and book you for an
    oil change as well.
But for now she needs to schedule you for repairs to remove that
    broomstick the scarecrow shoved up your ass.
But she will never tell.

What's that smell?

Take a look around you. Do you smell it in the air?
People pushing and shoving without a single care.
The rudeness and aggression are, at least to me, more common place.
Some ass out of control and up in your face.
The ones that can do no wrong and not take instruction well.
The ones that will never learn and will burn in hell.
The country that I once loved is burning to the ground.
Don't you see and smell it? Just take a look around.
There is beauty too, but apparently getting much harder to see.
Because the world has been blinded by greed and lust. It's not about you, it's all about me.
The common man doesn't stand a chance as he tries to stand his ground.
Can't you smell it in the air? Just take a look around.
People in a hurry. No courtesy anymore.
No equal slice of the pie. It's all about me, not you attitude for sure.
What happened to our country? Has it always been this way?
I look back at history of the wars we have fought and yes, it's all I have to say.

Under Water

What do I do my Lord? I think of it almost every day.
Now that I'm old with a head and face of gray.
My house in underwater and my bills are out of sight.
I am sick and old and must keep working to make things right.
Down to a two day work week, not enough to cover my bills.
Please Lord, give me some answers here. I'm already living my life
    without any thrills.
I'm too sick to work one job, yet alone work two.
Please Lord answer me, I don't know what to do.
I have down sized my life already. How much more can I cut?
I feel the cuts I make every day when I have to fill my gut.
Please Lord, help me keep my home.
I am sick and way to old not to have a place to call my own.
I was young once and did not plan my life so well.
Now I'm old and sick. Please Lord help me so I do not have to sell.
I bought my home when most people including myself were doing
    okay.
Please Lord help me help me keep afloat. I don't know what else
    to say.

What does God Say?

This poem may or may not be all that politically correct; it's not for
    me to say.

But I do know what God says in his word the Holy Bible; that he
    doesn't think much about lesbians or gays.

You see society seems to except it and the churches have all
    joined in.

I don't think that's what God says. He thinks it is a sin.

God took a rib from Adam so he can have a mate named Eve.

He never intended at any time for her to be called Steve.

Wherefore a man shall take unto himself a bride and they shall
    become as one flesh.

Not man on man or woman on woman tangled in the devils mesh.

The devil has convinced modern man that it is okay to live this way.

I think people should listen more to what God and his Holy Bible has
    to say.

It was not how God intended it for a man to burn with desire for
    another man.

It was never meant to be, it was never in the plan.

Woman was created for man, not for one another.

God says shame on you, as you displease him and your mother.

Price of a Drink

All your prizes and possessions won't mean much when you are
dead.
Just monuments of what you achieved while here on earth.
Where will you go and what will they be worth?
You work all your life to acquire all that gold.
What is it worth when you lay there in your coffin and your bones are
cold.
You stand at those gates with all your gold.
And you hear your gold is worthless here so you are told.
Maybe it will buy you a drink, way down there below.
So you pack up all your gold, and off you go.
Please Mr. Devil, will you let me in?
Of course I will. Your gold is always good here.
Now who wins as you think?
"Come on over here." The Devil says "Sit down here at the bar; let
me pour you a drink."
You sit and you chat. You tell of all you achieved and did.
And then ask "Where's the bathroom?" "I need to lift a lid."
"Over there!" "Don't forget to flush!"
So off you go in a mighty rush.
As you finish your business and pull the plunger. You're relieved with
a shout.
As the floor of the bathroom begins to fall out.
You're screaming and falling into a fiery place.
Because all that gold did not buy that smile off of Satin's face.

Thank you Note

I'm not so bright, but I know God shines on me in his own
   special way.
I do my best to praise him and give him the glory every day.
Without him, I am nothing he gives me what I need to live.
And if there if abundance, there is always more to give.
The Devil tries his best to make me stumble with his evil ways.
But I bow my head and I am humble and I begin to pray.
Lord, give me strength and wisdom to quench those fiery darts from
   hell.
To speak the words that you give me to break the wicked spell.
No I'm not the brightest nor do I have a golden tongue.
But I know that I am saved from an eternity of burning and why God
   gave his son.

Swords Edges

I've seen the evil. I've seen the wicked.

I have battled each in their own special way.

I put on my armor and fight the poisonous darts and sharpen my
sword every day.

What a battle, I am weakened and I am tired, but victorious none the
less.

As Satan tries with his demons to put me through his test.

His army is strong and many. He knows the battle plan well.

But when Christ returns for his chosen saints; Satan will burn in Hell.

How long is eternity? A pretty long time I would say.

So until the roll call is called by Christ my lord, Ill sharpen my sword
every day.

I'll keep fighting those demons. They seem to be everywhere these
days.

He put up a very good fight, as you fight his wicked ways.

Please Lord, return soon. My swords edges are wearing down.

As I fight another demon and kick his ass out of town.

Diabetes

The sugar in my blood is way out of control.

As I take another slice and have another roll.

You count those carbs, you take those pills and you really feel like hell.

You just want to feel better, but only time will tell.

The quack says to lose some weight; I wish he knew where I'm at.

That's easier said than done, as you cut off that fat.

You stroll past the cupcakes and candy. You know you can't have any at all.

Because you know if you do you will feel like hell and start to climb a wall.

Why do my legs hurt so much? It's sure getting hard to walkabout.

That cake you made sure was good. Now you lay in your bed and scream and shout.

Why am I so tired? I can hardly stay awake.

Damn that birthday party with the ice cream and cake.

You lay in bed and can't sleep as you toss and turn.

Why the hell can't you say no to that sweet tooth? When the hell will you learn?

L.A. Road Trip

She was just thirteen I believe at that time.
When we took a road trip to L.A. in that truck of mine.
Not really my truck I drive it for some other turd.
As the miles past from that country town listening to my every word.
Just a child not a clue to the world and of its ways.
Talking on the C.B. to the other drivers and learning what they had
     to say.
Are we there yet? How much farther do we have to go?
Go get some sleep in the sleeper. I will let you know.
I took the truck down town where the wine'os, homeless and
     prostitutes hung out.
As she hung her head out the window like a puppy looking all about.
That's a transvestite over there. "What's that?" she says.
So I say a man in a dress as we drive by and she glares.
Here's a prostitute! I don't need to explain that to you.
"She's so pretty." She says "How would you have known?"
Well the class room drive by had to be a lesson all of its own.
For that thirteen year old niece Chester, it was the best time she had
     ever been shown.

Last Respect

The morgue just called. Can you please come in and identify a
 corpse?
Yes, I'll be right there, of course.
Yes, that's my daughter. I can tell by that tattoo right there.
Why did she do it? Why did she not care?
They found pills and alcohol in her room I'm told.
Yes, I'm not surprised. She has been an addict since she was thirteen
 years old.
We are sorry they say as tears roll down my face.
This should never have happened. It seems so out of place.
The booze and drugs consumed her. She couldn't lose that monkey
 on her back.
She was never able to say no to a party or a line of crack.
She couldn't say no. She would always partake.
Now her family gathers to pay their last respect at the church for her
 wake.
She wasn't really a bad girl. She just liked her drugs and booze.
Now her family hangs their heads to cry, as they lay her to rest
 because now they are the ones that lose.

Endorphins

When the endorphin high is over from all the drugs and sex,
Who and what will you cross off the list? What will you try next?
From all you have done in your life I'm surprised there is a living
    brain cell to excite.
But you always manage to push the envelope a little farther as you
    push with all your might.
What is your goal? Perhaps to see your head explode.
As you search and prowl in the dark, waiting to unload.
You will find that next high. The endorphins won't let you down.
As the high you get keeps stealing a little more from those cells
    within your brain, as they catch the next bus out of town.
Those endorphins will leave you empty and without a place to call
    home.
As you keep looking for that next high. I'm sure you're not alone.
Those endorphins will keep you satisfied; at least temporarily.
When and what will it take before you finally see?
The endorphins will always want more as it feeds upon itself.
As you ran-sack through your purse for those pills and grab the
    Vodka off the shelf.
You are always looking for that endorphin rush with your drugs and
    your booze.
But when the rush is over, you're the one to lose.

Apology

Gee dad, I'm sorry for not seeing things your way.
Now my eyes are opened; I don't know what to say.
Gee dad, I'm sorry for all that I have put you through.
I am sorry I didn't see. I wish that somehow I would have knew.
Gee dad thank you for all that you have done for me.
Why was I so blind, why did I not see?
Gee dad I'm sorry for all the pain I caused you and the sacrifices you
    endured.
I'm sorry for what I put you through while you were hoping and
    waiting to be cured.
I see how you have suffered and endured for me in so many ways.
Gee Dad I'm sorry and don't know what to say.
You sold the things you loved to help me with my life.
Gee Dad, I'm sorry that I caused you all that pain and added to your
    strife,
You tried your best to counsel me and show me a better way.
I am sorry dad and don't know what to say.
You gave me the tools and pointed to what path to follow.
But I didn't listen to you. Now my humility I must swallow.
Will you accept my apology for what I have put you through?
My heart and eyes were blind I wish I would have knew.
I'm sorry I stole from you so I could get high.
I'm sorry dad, now my eyes are open and I wonder why.
The things you treasured, that you will never see again. That I sold
    for a high because my life was a whirlwind.
Please accept my heartfelt apology Dad. I'm sorry you're hurt and
    shamed.
Gee Dad I am sorry and the one who should be blamed.

Tic Toc Tic

Where have all the memories gone? Stored somewhere within my
mind.
Age has robbed me of my youth. It hasn't been all that kind.
Who will come and help me when I can do no more?
When my body is weak and sick with age and feeling mighty sore.
When the simple things that once were easy. I cannot do without
some help from someone else's hands.
Because I am old and feeble now and find it hard to stand.
When once my independence defined my character of whom I
thought I was.
Now I am weak with age and sickness. I don't like it all that much.
How we aged not knowing of the future. Knowing you can't turn back
the clock.
Now you are old and feeble and find it difficult to stand and walk.
You have seen and done many things when young while the clock of
time clicks away.
Now you reflect the memories of distant times. Never thinking of the
future and the price you would pay.
Think and plan your life. Stay healthy if you can.
Take it from this once strong but now aged, feeble, broke and worn
out old man.

The Goose Just Died

Take nothing for granted. For what you have now, thank God
    every day.
Because the way things are going it could all just blow away.
We are a nation of abusers. We think that golden goose will
    never die.
How many do you see give thanks to the true God and are humble
    to the spirit somewhere upon high?
Most people you see can't live within their means.
New cars in the driveway and living on a dream.
That goose won't live forever, but they will feed and pamper it well.
How long will it live? I guess time will only tell.
I believe that a time is coming when that goose shall lay no more,
When the creditors are calling and knocking at your door.
When the gold is all gone and the plastic won't buy a loaf of bread.
Because this is what was foretold by prophets and what the Holy
    Bible said.
When man shall fight one another for that loaf of bread.
But I thank my God and I am humble because he will call his saints
    and raise his faithful from the dead.

Inscription

How will you remember me when I am gone and you read an
inscription upon a stone?

When you are standing in remembrance of the things said and done
and you're all alone.

Will I be remembered as a good man or the ass you always thought I
was? Will you shed a tear?

Will you know now why you are free and will you hold it dear?

Will you remember all he had done for you to get to know the child
he lost so long ago?

Will you remember how you used it to your advantage and had so
little of yourself to show?

Will you remember me through my art pieces while you hold them
dear?

Will you think of all the work it took while you shed that tear?

While I was alive you showed me what your treasures were and what
you seemed to want along with wealth.

The things you desired and lusted for were gold and silver, but what
you thought about was yourself.

Over Cooked

I've seasoned hard, my heart is cold.
I hate to say it, but now I'm old.
With each new season comes growth and death.
To watch something grow and die and take its last breath,
Like a mighty oak tree it started so small.
And with time and age, gave shade for us all.
The seasoning of a man is much the same way.
You grow and you learn of your life as you put on your pants and
    coat each new day.
The things we see and do shape and mold us to the person we seem
    to be.
Like the small acorn seed to the mighty oak tree.
We season in time. We mature as we go.
With knowledge and a little bit of wisdom that we try to show.
The process of life is simple, just look at God's plan.
From infant to child and then to a man.
Learning God's will for us all and doing the best we can.
I've seasoned hard like an old strip of leather.
Left out on the fence in the rain, wind and all sorts of weather.
It's cracked and hard like my heart and my face.
Not always secure of who I am and feeling at times out of place.
Like my life and that old saddle; it has been used and seasoned with
    time.
And has many stories to tell of life's twists and turns and we learn it is
    not always so kind.
But it is the process of life we all must endure.
Hoping and praying for our Lord's return on that we can be sure.

Paint and Feathers

I understand the pecking order of life and that it can be a little rough.
Does that explain your behavior as Top Dog or why you're so tough?
Okay, I get it! You're Top Dog, the one that has to be seen.
A prick and an ass and always quite mean.
I don't care about your war paint or bonnet or the tales you have
     spun.
I get it! You're the chief and have to be number 1.
You sit low on your thrown and bark; Come on look at me.
I get it! You're the chief and want everyone to see.
There will always be a new dog to challenge that top dog spot.
Will you always be ready for the fight to show this pup what
     you've got?
Perhaps the pup should win this fight! What then would you say?
As you stand there naked upon your thrown and your Top Dog title is
     taken away.
I get it! You're number 1. You should humble yourself to your tribe.
Try to be a leader… Throw away the war paint and bonnet… and
     stop trying to hide.
So as you stand there naked, stripped of all your glory and fame;
Will you hang your head and be humble and hang your head in
     shame?
Did the war paint and feathers really define you as a man?
As you stand before your band of followers reflecting your life's span.

Bully

What you can't take it? You can't play in the big boy store?
You're a little taken back and your ass is a little sore?
You should toughen up… have skin like an alligators hide.
What, you can't take it and you want off of this ride?
Life is going to throw those darts at you. You need to stand firm and
    stand your ground.
Roll with the punches… throw some back if needed to show you are
    sound.
The bullies will always be there thinking their better than the rest.
Throwing those darts to get at you to see if you pass his test.
The bully wants you to think he's tough and can frighten you to run
    and hide.
That's the joy he gets because he wants the recognition for the price
    of his ride.
He thinks his actions defines who he is by what he does and how he
    thinks.
But those actions paint a white stripe down his back because this
    person really stinks.
Most people don't and can't take the time to take a check-up from
    the neck up and ask just how I am perceived by the ones I touch.
If they did, maybe we would have a better world to live in because the
    ass in all of us in not liked all that much.

Future! What Future?

Who would have thought I should live this long. It certainly was
not me.
Now I am old and wear readers just to see.
We were all young once; some of you still are.
My advice for you youngster is have a clear vision for your future and
let it take you far.
If you think you won't grow old and have a set plan in place.
You will wonder as you look into the mirror and see the gray upon
your head and face.
Time has a way of catching up to you once you begin to get that
head of gray.
You look back and wonder where in the hell the time went the events
that changed that hair from brown to gray.
So as I lay here in my office thinking of what might happen next.
Because I didn't plan for my future. But I have passed all of life's
torturous tests.
Time has its ups and downs like the cogs within a wheel.
Events and time shape the soul, but age makes it hard to heal.
I've done my best. I've paid my dues. I'll die knowing that I tried.
I have done lots of wrong, but asked for forgiveness and yes, we all
have lied.
So plan your life you youngsters because youth will not be all fun and
games.
You too shall grow old. Will you be ready and prepared when the
Lord shall call your name?

Drugs, Booze and a Crashed Car

I guess we will see the outcome of your latest scenario;
Of how the cards play out and where you will go.
You broke the contract. I see now who you really are.
As your addictions keep consuming your soul and you crash
another car.
You would think by now that living clean and sober would be a better
way to live.
You have cheated, stolen and lied to everyone; they have nothing left
to give.
What are you thinking now as you are sitting hand cuffed in the back
seat of a police car.
Did you think the drugs and booze would fuel that stolen vehicle and
take you all that far?
You have lived a life of booze and drugs that have cost you and your
family much hurt and shame.
But as soon as you get free you think everyone else is to blame.
What is wrong with you? Why can't you be responsible, keep a job
and settle down?
All of your shenanigans seem to always catch up to you as the lynch
mob tries to catch you as your hauling ass out of town.
You got away once more. Are there more aces hid up your sleeve?
As you cheat, steal and lie your entire life because you are a common
thief.
You have hid many times, but this time you got caught.
Now you're headed back to jail and then prison because you give
your life little thought.
You will have plenty time to think and sober up and while the time
away;
Think of how life was when you were clean and sober and of a
brighter day.

Moving Day

I am a simple old man just trying to get by.

With a dysfunctional child that says I often make her cry.

Maybe sobriety would help you. You should give it a try.

The truth hurts doesn't it and that is why you cry.

My answer to you is simple, but I shake my head and wonder why.

I have given you the tools and pointed you in the right direction.

But like before, you simply cannot make the connection.

You are smart and have the looks that will get you what you need.

Your biggest problem is your addictions you can't play by the rules of
life because you pay no heed.

I don't understand you and clearly you don't understand what I have
to say.

As you're led away in a police car to your new residence with bars of
steel that are painted gray.

When will you see that your addictions change your behavior?

Get clean and stay sober. Plan for a brighter day and better weather.

You don't humble yourself to instruction or correction all that well.

Perhaps you will now as you are led away to your new home called
the Gray Bar Hotel.

A Long Road to Travel

It has been a long trip I think I'll sit down and hang up my hat.
Reflect of what has brought me to this point and time and try to see
where I'm at.
The road has been long and not at all easy going.
I have put the past miles behind me now, but the future is of not
always knowing.
The things we see and do as we travel this long and well-traveled
road.
The ups and downs in life as we try to haul the load.
The things that come with the journey that define who and what
we are.
The journey has been long and hard and has taken me very far.
The load has not always been light. The pay has not been so great.
As I approach the final destination now that I am old and
approaching heaven's gates.
I'll get in line to talk to the dock worker and hope he will hear what I
have to say.
As I convers of my long journey and he then sends me on my way.
Will I get a back haul or be sent somewhere south and hot? Perhaps
not on the route.
Because the dispatcher didn't like the last road I took, as he screams
and shouts.
Well my next dispatch was my last one apparently I'm no longer
needed for the haul.
I get to stay here at these pearly gates with Jesus
and now salute all of those trips with my one finger and say God
bless them all.

The Past is Gone

As I reflect the memories of my life and of the past.

I think of the future and wonder will these hard times last?

People out of work, politicians saying the recession is over and things are picking up.

I'm sorry I just don't see it at the pumps when I go to put gas in my truck.

Things seemed slower when I was young. People seemed to care for each other a little more.

You could go and do more with a dollar and didn't have to lock your door.

If you needed it your neighbor had it and would gladly lend a hand.

What happened to our country and this once great land?

I look around me and see that kids don't have a clue.

Talking and texting on their devices with no thought or respect for me and you.

Every other house in foreclosure; how are we to survive?

Just trying to keep my head above the water, pay what bills I can to stay alive.

That's for the ones that are working there are still plenty that are not.

Although my life is meager I am thankful for what I've got.

I do my best to be charitable and help the ones I know in need.

Because I know God will provide for the ones who need it and Satan for the ones with greed.

Dead Presidents

What would you do tomorrow if what you had today just blew away?
The things you need and use each day that help you on your way.
If you bank account was useless, the bank just folded up.
No more coffee at Starbucks or water in your cup.
The things you take for granted that you cannot live without.
Who will you blame? Will you scream and shout?
No water for a shower or to flush a turd.
Nothing for the trees or lawn; now isn't this absurd?
You're in disbelief. How can this be taken place?
When your dollar is useless and that old George Washington hangs
     his head with disgrace.
We spent like drunken sailors thinking the good times and money
     would never die.
Because our government could always print some more and it
     wouldn't lie.
Once the super power of the world; hated by foreign soil.
Sold out to Okmed for that damned barrel of oil.
Okmed and Chen Yang own this country. Now what do you do?
When that old dollar bill in your wallet won't buy a shoe lace for your
     worn out shoe.
When you are standing in a soup line for a cup of soup and a slice of
     bread;
Will you take heed now to what God in his Holy Bible said?
Or will you go about life in its unusual way.
Wondering how this happened and wondering what to say.
Harken to these words written perhaps by a prophet of modern
     times.
There just might be a message hidden between the lines.

Regrets and Fear

What regrets do you have because you did not take that chance?
A career, a hidden challenge, or a lost romance.
Have your fears and regrets justified the pain you felt?
Because you never took that chance; you thought your fate was with
    the hand you were dealt.
Was it fear of rejection or fear of another form or fashion?
That may have delivered you to find a hidden passion.
You're stopped in your tracks; you shake from the fear.
Frozen in time, waiting for the boogie man to appear.
Fear is not always what it would appear to be;
Ways of self-defense till you wait and see.
Some forms of fear would be real; you are the judge.
Some things are best left alone to hold on to that grudge.

I'll Take That Bet

You didn't cover your assets. You were having too much fun.
Now you're broke and homeless and you're on the run.
Your life has crumbled like a biscuit left out in the rain.
The things that once were priceless are gone. I'm sure there is some
    shame.
The creditors want your assets. You're way over with your debts.
You were having too much fun to cover your bills when you made
    another bet.
The realities of life are wicked when faced with day to day.
As you have that second drink then run off to play.
Is this the life you envisioned? Is it what you had in mind?
Never any money; broke and homeless because life is not that kind.
Life is not that fun my friend, but it is better that you would think.
As you place another bet and the bartender pours you another drink.
If you focused on your debt and poured that bottle down the sink;
Sobered up and stayed that way. Life would get better for you. Surely
    I would think!

The Battle

The battle is over, this day is done. I lay my armor down and I rest.

To regain my strength to fight another day of all of Satan's evil tests.

David slew a giant with a stone. Sampson killed thousands with a jaw
bone of an ass.

My battles are small, but mighty to me. As I watch each new day
pass.

God delivered them from their enemies and concurred Satan
through their hands.

And gave them strength to fight another day as they fought to take
their stand.

I ask my God to deliver me from each new affliction that I must
endure.

Knowing that I am victorious with God's spirit working through me to
make my mind and body pure.

Those days were fought with shed blood. Christ my Lord shed his
blood for all.

I do my best to fight each new battle because I have risen to his call.

Your Calling

When the trump is call up yonder and you're standing naked all
    alone.
When the book of life is opened and your life is shown.
As you stand there humble shaking at your knees.
Sorry for your life and the things you've done, because you refuse to
    listen or believe.
Now your life is over and you're bound for hell.
Your evil lies have fooled many with the stories that you tell.
That crooked smile you wear tells your story with your tongue being
    sharp and bitter with the stench of a stiff hard drink.
You're an evil wicked man and your life it truly stinks.
Of the hate and guile you lived by of the wickedness in your heart.
Dark, cold and hardened; to blind to depart.

Bad Ass President

Mr. President, do you have a clue to what is going on around you?

I'm sure all of your advisors are pulling all your strings as you play your role so well.

Or is it really just your song and dance? I don't know. It's really hard for me to tell.

I see your lips are moving but all I hear are lies.

You need to wipe the bullshit off your lips before it attracts the flies.

How are we as a nation supposed to believe everything we see or hear?

When all I see in my neighborhood are the foreclosed homes and homeless people; I hang my head and shed a tear.

Empty campaign promises, you sing and dance so well.

Are we as a nation to feel the pain of four more years of misery while our country goes to hell?

You live in your white castle while the country pays your rent.

Are you earning your wages with your song and dance routine?

Is our money being well spent?

If I were to perform my job as poorly as you are,

I would be fired and the repo man then would take my car.

Wake up Mr. President, our country is bleeding and is falling apart.

Your bandage policies and your lies are killing a nation that I believe once had a pulse,

But now it lacks the heart.

I see no confidence in this land, of its people that were once proud and free.

Our government and its leaders are all consumed by their titles and their greed to care anything about you and me.

So Mr. President, I hope you have enjoyed all your perks.

As you take another vacation while this country has to work.

So you can fly here and there and do as you seem fit and this country pays the bills.

For me, Mr. President, I am trying to pay me mortgage each month with no money in the pot for any other thrills.

Reflections Through a Windshield

All though the wheels are turning there is seldom anywhere to go.
As you try to climb the ladder fighting the wind, the rain and snow.
You have done this for over thirty years and have only climbed to that
    first rung in the ladder.
Now you are older but not much smarter, as you look for a place to
    pull over to relieve your bladder.
This is it you won't go any farther.
You better settle in, because there is really no need to bother
You chose the wrong career. You were expecting wealth and fame.
You really have no one but yourself to credit for that mistake or no
    one else to blame.
Without that education you had little to choose from or take stock.
Now you're older and you reflect on how the time turned with those
    wheels in motion; like an eight day clock.
What do you have you've scrimped and saved for everything
    you own.
A house and three dogs, but your all alone.
Not much to claim; now it's all downhill from here.
Will you make it to the finish line with just a little over a year?
Sixty-one and counting until I can pull the plug and retire.
Will I be able to live a life then and be able to do the things that I
    desire?

Summer Outing

Do you remember the good ol days when life didn't seem so hard?
When you could play cowboy and Indians without any worries in your
  back yard.
When you didn't have to lock your doors for fear of someone
  breaking in to steal you blind.
Things seemed to be a little slower then and people were somewhat
  more kind.
Crime wasn't so prevalent, but it was still there.
Times were more pleasant then when people seemed to care.
I remember summer outings and fishing at some stream.
Lying in the grass with the shade of a cotton wood tree while I drifted
  off to dream.
I remember the lunches that my mother made of peanut butter and
  jelly
and a thermos with some hot soup to warm our belly.
I remember we would all pile in dad's pick-up truck with our dog and
  go on a drive out in the hills.
We didn't have much money, but this was how we got our thrills.
A day spent together with one another and functioning the best that
  we could.
Making memories that would last a lifetime out in the hills looking for
  a fossil or a piece of petrified wood.
These were the times of my life learning to appreciate nature at its
  best.
Now I am old I reflect, as I have been put through life's mighty test.
Time spent as a family, yes, we had our trying times,
but life seemed a lot easier then and just a little more fine.

Dysfunction

A dysfunctional family, where did it start?

A lifetime of anguish with many broken hearts.

The fights, the drama, the emotions of feelings destroyed with words,
with a style.

You try and try again to piece the puzzle together to make any sense
of the hurt it has caused trial after trial.

You watch and you learn because this is how it is taught.

As family after family dies from the rot.

The cycle must be recognized, and then it must be broken.

A change from the heart, with God's word being spoken.

A family divided cannot build its future on solid soil.

A lifetime of dysfunction is put to the toil.

Change must take place and start with God at the head.

Before it's too late and another dysfunctional family lies dead.

Plan Now

I know the things I must do to see it to the end.

The cutting and splitting of my winter wood; the money I must
spend.

The fixing of that roof that leaks to keep the rain at bay.

To keep me dry and warm inside my house for that better day.

I have to think it through. Planning is a must.

There is no one else that I can rely on to get it done. I'm the only one
to trust.

You can learn a lot from an insect. The ants spend all spring and
summer gathering for their winter needs.

They know that fall then winter comes and you must take heed.

You must stock up now and plan for that day tomorrow.

For when you're cold and hungry because you didn't plan and hang
your head with sorrow.

Stone Face

They called him stone face expressionless, hard hearted, cold, and
    all alone.
Not expressing love because too little was ever shown.
He did not smile much for the afflictions he endured.
Often wondering why or if there was a cure.
He stood fast on his beliefs, concreted, solid in his ways.
Honest with the words he spoke, seldom would he stray.
Quite often a loner, not one to stand out in a crowd.
Soft spoken and easy going with his message; never was he proud.
Willing to help some stranger that had some sort of need.
Often to see of the self-motivation behind the cause of their greed.
Some are talkers, come are listeners. Stone face had little to say.
He would rather listen to others brag and boast about themselves
    then go about his way.
Stone face had no one to help him to get it done. His dogs were his
    companions.
Self-sufficient and self-reliant he was the only one.
Little did he have, but what he had he gave.
To be taken advantage of and abused till the time he was laid to his
    grave.

Asphalt Rail

I'm an engineer on the asphalt rail that passes through our land.
I've carried loads from coast to coast and walked upon those coastal
  sands.
I've run that rail with wheels of rubber. Hauling the freight this
  country needs.
I've traveled many miles on that asphalt rail as people paid no heed.
I've seen the faces of our cities that are tied together with that
  asphalt bow.
And trucks stacked up like dominos at the loading docks nicely in
  a row.
I've used the backs of those frames of steel to get those loads from
  here to there.
I've made those deliveries on time with little thanks at all that
  dispatcher seldom cared.
I've seen those cold snowy winter passes and scorching heat
  and sun.
Wondering what's in store for me down the asphalt rail as I call for
  my next run.
I've watched that sunset on a landscape of saguaro cactus with heat
  waves rising off that asphalt rail.
While off in the distance you see a lake that is not there.
Those waves of heat playing tricks on your mind saying try me if you
  dare.
I've put those wheels of rubber through some trying times.
Miles of ice and snow, rain and wind, and made it home just fine.

Princess Queen

The princess puts her makeup on then goes out to play all night.
Something is going on here that just doesn't feel right.
How do you expect to win my respect and love, when all you do
is lie?
I ask myself what is the reasoning behind your secrecy; I ask the
question why.
What is going on here I sense you're up to no good.
You stay out all night then sleep all day, while I have to stack the
wood.
I work all day to pay the bills then come home with the house a
mess.
While you chat to your friends all day on Facebook. Then I have to
deal with the drama and the stress.
You're just a child learning of life and its evil tricks.
You're afraid to admit your guilt as you take those nasty licks.
If you could review the book of your life opened to your page;
The events and situations that you dealt with, with your fits of rage.
The battles you lost have been many; oh the tears you've shed.
How many more will you cry before you wake up dead?

Dancing Partner

You've been dancing with the devil. I think you know what I mean.
Doing the wrong things at the right time most of your life; as though
      it would seem.
He always seems to hurt you and always let you down.
When you think you need him the most, he is never to be found.
You gave him everything you had to satisfy that longing in your heart.
While he left you cold and lonely…empty, to broke to make that new
      start.
Not the friend or companion you could count on when the chips
      were down, unreliable, untrusting, and never to be found.
But somehow you put your trust in him. When will you see?
He controls your heart and soul, and will not set you free.
I think that you should find a new dancing partner. I know someone
      you should get to know.
A kind and gentle man that has plenty to give and show.
They call him a king, a Lord, and a Savior.
Maybe you should give him a call. Perhaps he could help you with
      your bad behavior.
They say he has done miracles. Perhaps he could help you too.
I'll give you his number. You should give him a call if you choose.
I wrote his number down within this book.
You can have it when you're ready to make that call and take a look.

Nightmare

Our world seems to be falling apart; quite literally at the seams.
Earthquakes, pestilence, war and famine; tell me it's a dream.
When I wake up will it all be over? Will we be living and loving one
   another?
Or shall I return unto this nightmare and crawl back underneath
   these covers.
To be awakened by a frightful sight; to wake up with a scream.
Frozen under those covers unable to move; was it but a dream?
Shaken by the nightmare trying to make those pictures in my mind
   disappear;
But they are forever in my memory; real and always there.

Cover Your Assets

You didn't cover your assets; you were having too much fun.
Now you're broke, homeless, and you're on the run.
Your life has crumbled like a biscuit left in the rain.
The things that once were priceless are gone. I'm sure there's some
    shame.
The creditors want your assets; you're way over with your debt.
You were having too much fun to cover your bills when you made
    that bet.
The realities of life are wicked when forced with day to day.
As you have that second drink then run off to play.
Is this the life you envisioned? Is it what you had in mind?
Never any money, broke, and homeless; because life is not that kind.

Freedom's Price

Enjoy your freedom it has come with a mighty cost.
Don't take it for granted. Many a life was lost.
Enjoy the things it has to offer you. There are many that can't and
    never will.
Many are oppressed and fighting for it still.
Enjoy what you have, but never forget the price that was paid.
To do the things you love with the freedom we inherit from the
    warrior who fought and died with the sacrifice he made.

Daughter of Perdition

You're quite lacking in the morals department oh daughter of
    perdition.
Void of judgment with your reprobate mind of which you've been
    given.
When it comes to right from wrong your mind becomes quite hazy.
To you, you take the serpent's way because he has taught you to be
    lazy.
It's easier for you to take that of what you never worked for or earned
    with your own hands.
Oh they will never miss it. She will never wear that pearl strand.
You oh devil's prodigy, you know all of Satan's games.
He has taken control of your mind and soul. Do you feel no shame?
You seem to think nothing of the torture of your victims; it's all part
    of your evil plot.
To get what you can steal from others, while your soul rots.

T-Rex

Burry me with ol' T-Rex; a relic of the past.
Now, I too, am ancient and life seems way too fast.
Instant information with the tough of a phone.
Burry me with ol' T-Rex so he isn't all alone.
Time sure is different now, compared to way back when.
I'll ponder the old days while I sip upon my gin.
Where did the time go; rusted with the weather?
Burry me with ol' T-Rex so our bones will be together.
Fossils are a remembrance left as clues to remember.
Of how times and events were recorded when T-Rex and I were
      together.
Ol' T-Rex was my companion, my buddy and my friend.
Always loyal and with me to the end.
He died in his sleep. I sure hope that is how I go.
But, burry me with my old dog T-Rex. Of that time, I just don't know.

Wish of Two Fathers

All you had to do is listen to the words of wisdom spoken.

From an aged old broken man that in his heart hoping.

Trying to direct a path that leads to a life of destruction and an empty heart.

Hoping you would see and know of the evil that surrounds your soul for you to, make that new start.

Not to put your trust in man but of your Lord above,

And know that he will direct your path and adorn you with his love.

Seek him and he will answer you in his own special way.

Know that he is with you and he will help you not to stray.

Talk to him daily. That is all he asks of you.

He is your heavenly father. I think it is something you can do.

Like your earthly father all he wants is your respect and love.

Be humble and talk to us; all we wish is to see you rise above.

You break both our hearts to see you live the way you are.

Because you don't see the evil of Satan's darkness and why he won't let you go that far.

Open your eyes and heart. It is really easy to see.

How Satan's grip controls your life and he will not set you free.

Ask and he shall deliver, seek and you will find.

The power of love from God above; there is really no other kind.

Tell him your desires not of your wants and greed.

He will listen that's his job. He will always fill your need.

But you must take the action. Get off your ass and keep trying.

Because Satan won't stop unless you tell him to; he will keep on lying.

I often think about the twists and turns that my life has taken to bring me where I am now with my life. Life teaches us many things. You have to do your own living to learn and hopefully grow from all the experiences that your life's path will take you down. The older you get seems to let you know and reflect the good, the bad and the in between moments of your life. You seldom know when you have done something right, but you always know when something goes to crap. It is those crap moments that sometimes you wish you could have, should have, by some other means done the right thing in the first place, but at the moment of the event, you never knew what the right thing might have been. That is the learning point; to see and wonder what, when, who, why, and how the event went wrong and what I must learn from it.

I'm personally a slow learner. Don't ask me why. I've always have been. A.D.D., yeah, most likely. It doesn't make me all bad. I do have my moments.

We are all here to learn and do God's will; to teach the gospel and of the son of God, Jesus Christ. That is what we are supposed to do.

But in the meantime, things and life evolve so it seems. Eventually, for the condition of the world that God has been far removed from people's lives; and that is exactly what Satan wants.

Until people get back to knowing God's word and the true power that controls the events on earth; little can be changed until the return of Jesus Christ.

Printed in the United States
By Bookmasters